FUNNY THINGS HAPPENED:

FROM BRIGHTON
TO BOCA

FUNNY THINGS HAPPENED:

FROM BRIGHTON TO BOCA

A Memoir by George Karp

Columbus, Ohio

FUNNY THINGS HAPPENED:
FROM BRIGHTON TO BOCA

Published by Gatekeeper Press

2167 Stringtown Rd, Suite 109

Columbus, OH 43123-2989

www.GatekeeperPress.com

ISBN: 9781642371000

eISBN: 9781642371017

Printed in the United States of America

I am dedicating this book to my late wife,

Rita Bari Karp.

Acknowledgements

I would like to acknowledge the many people who inspired me to write this memoir, my first book. My children Jennifer, Heather, and Vanessa, and my sister Arlene, all were instrumental in my writing and were totally supportive of me. My son-in-law, Mark, gave me many great ideas in putting together this masterpiece! My many friends pushed me towards reaching my literary goal. I would like to thank my editor, Barbara Cronie, of Editing Par Excellence for guiding me down the highway to successfully completing my story.

Thanks again, all.

Yesterday is history — tomorrow is a mystery — today is a gift of God, which is why we call it the present.

Contents

INTRODUCTION:

THE WORLD ACCORDING TO KARP

CAN YOU IMAGINE if Frank Sinatra, Barbra Streisand, or Elton John started their singing careers at age 78? What if Babe Ruth, Serena Williams, or Lebron James first picked up a ball at age 78? How about if Ernest Hemingway, John Steinbeck, or F. Scott Fitzgerald began to write at age 78? That would be truly incredulous! Well, here I am at age 78 writing my memoir,

Funny Things Happened : From Brighton to Boca.

Now I know that I am not a Sinatra, a Babe Ruth or a Hemingway, and I know that I am not a legend in my own mind. But, I have lived a long life; I have a great memory and I have had a lot of experiences, both funny and sad that I would like to put on paper. Most of this book will tell of my funny experiences. I hope that you will find these humorous. I tell people or whoever will listen that I remember every day of my life.

One may ask just for whom am I writing this book? I am writing this for my three terrific daughters, Jennifer, Heather, and Vanessa and their super husbands, Mark, Jordan, and Darryl and my five wonderful grandchildren, Stella, Jeremy, Elizabeth, Conrad, and Evan. I am writing this for my loving sister Arlene and her great husband Harvey, their families, and for my ex-wife Kathy. My late great parents, Estelle and Jack, residing in heaven and always proud of their little boy, can now be proud of their big boy. Also hopefully, my many friends, both old and new, will read and enjoy this memoir. Most importantly, I am writing this for my late wife Rita, who I know is there for me spiritually, inspiring me to write and is correcting my grammar and spelling, just like she always did. Rita, I miss you!

I've been thinking about writing a book for a very long time. Originally, I planned to author a book about Brooklyn, my beloved

Dodgers, and my own personal life experiences. After Rita passed away, I was immersed into a new social life, and my thought was to write a book about senior dating and the amusing situations that I encountered, along with some personal anecdotes. While walking the dog one night (some of my best ideas come when I'm walking the dog), I realized that the best approach would be to write a book about my many humorous life experiences. It's 1,235 miles from Brighton Beach in Brooklyn, New York to Boca Raton, Florida — and so, *Funny Things Happened : From Brighton to Boca.* I hope you enjoy it!

First, a brief overview of my life, serious and not funny.

I was born February 10, 1939, the first child of Estelle and Jack Karp. My parents had been married seven years, but with the depression going on and hard times all around, the idea of a baby early in their marriage was not on their agenda. My folks were both born in Brooklyn, so I was born a second-generation Jewish American. My mom was twenty nine and my dad was thirty four when I arrived on the scene. My first home was in the Bensonhurst section of Brooklyn and we moved several times over the next few years. My mother's parents were Tillie (Lacritz) and Alfred Langer, both from somewhere in the Austro-Hungarian Empire. My father's parents were Katie (Gutter) and Max Karp, also having emigrated from the vast Austro-Hungarian Empire. My paternal grandmother Katie, whose name was really Gittle, died just before I was born and so I was named after her. Grandpa Alfred passed away when I was four. Grandpa Max became deceased when I was eleven, and Granny (my maternal grandmother) died when I was seventeen. I was fortunate to have thirteen first cousins.

Living in the Sheepshead Bay section of Brooklyn, I attended the Wee Wisdom Nursery School and graduated with honors. Now for the big time, I attended P.S. 254 and went there for three years. My sister Arlene was born in 1946 when I was seven and I was no longer an only child. When I was eight, we moved to Brighton 12th Street and there I developed my own Brighton Beach Memoirs. My new school, P.S. 225, was conveniently located across the street from our apartment house, with no need for a carpool (impossible, because we had no car and certainly no pool). At the old school, P.S. 254, I had few friends but in the new school, P.S. 225 and the new neighborhood, I developed many friendships. Soon after I transferred schools (in October), by February, I was elected class president of my fourth grade class. In fact, I was elected president in every grade until I graduated. I was not a great ballplayer, but I tried really hard, unsuccessfully, maybe just to impress my father. Modestly, I was a good student with high grades.

My mother was a quiet reserved person, just the opposite of my father, who was very outgoing and funny. My father was not a financial success, and both he and my mother had to work hard to support the family. Their marriage was great and I am proud to say that we had the *least* dysfunctional family that I have ever seen. My children tell me now that the stability that I acquired from my parents has filtered down to them which makes my children all solid citizens.

After graduating P.S.225 in 1952, I attended Abraham Lincoln High School for the next four years. In my first two years, I was an excellent student achieving a 93 percent average. I discovered girls in my junior year, and my active social life caused my academics to falter a bit. I pledged and joined the best fraternity in Lincoln and made many new friends. I won a New York State Regents scholarship for $1,400, which then was a huge amount of money. After graduation in 1956, I enrolled at City College of New York Uptown to study chemical engineering and after two days, I realized this school and curriculum were not for me. After one year at CCNY, I transferred to Brooklyn College to study chemistry. A year later, I realized that I did not want to be a scientist, so I transferred schools again, this time to CCNY Downtown (the Baruch School) to major in business. My social life interfered with my school life. If I had spent as much time at the library, instead of at my favorite hangout, Dubrows, I would have been a Rhodes Scholar! I graduated CCNY in 1961 and joined the Army reserves, (for six months active duty and six years in the reserves) serving in Fort Dix and Fort Sam Houston, where I became a medic.

In 1962, my cousin Bob was just going into the garment business for himself, and he offered me a job which I readily accepted. I loved the business and this was one of the happiest periods of my life. Being a social person, I dated a lot and then through a twist of fate in 1963,

I met Kathy Cassel. We dated for a year and got married in 1965. We lived in New York City and in 1967, Kathy was six months pregnant when my father suddenly died. Tragedy turned to happiness when my first child Jennifer was born. We lived in an apartment in Fort Lee, New Jersey, where daughter number two Heather was born in 1970 and then three years later Vanessa came into this world. My sister Arlene married Harvey Feldman during this period, and I became a partner in Bob's business and life was good. I started to play tennis at this time and tennis is still one of the great joys of my life. We bought a great house in Oradell, New Jersey, in 1974, which was the first house I had ever owned, and I loved it. Business was good; we traveled extensively and bought an apartment in Westhampton, Long Island, to use during the summer. We sold our house in Oradell, and moved to Great Neck (Kings Point), Long Island, to be closer to Westhampton. My mom got sick and passed away in 1980; then I was an orphan.

By 1984, I had become disenchanted with the garment business, and so at age 45, I retired for a while. The while was short-lived, and I became involved in Real Estate, becoming a vice president of Helmsley Spear two years later. My children were now in college or preparing to go to college, Jennifer at Tulane (and then Cardozo Law School), Heather at Boston University, and Vanessa at Wisconsin. Meanwhile, my twenty-seven year marriage was starting to dissipate, and I realized that I no longer wanted to be in New York and endure the cold weather. In 1992, as a single man, I moved to Boca Raton, Florida, not knowing what I really wanted to do with the rest of my life.

I met Rita Bari in 1993, married her seven years later and we were together for exactly twenty years, until her untimely death. I chose to go into the financial business, joining A.G. Edwards as a stock broker/financial adviser. I became a Certified Financial Planner and after ten years, I joined Barry Kaye Associates, leaders in the insurance industry. My three girls were now all married with children, living in New York, New Jersey, and California. Tragedy struck in 2013 when Rita suddenly and unexpectedly passed away. My children and sister were totally supportive of me during this horrible period, and I am eternally grateful to them. I officially retired in 2014 from business and now spend my time playing tennis, reading several newspapers each day, taking courses at Florida Atlantic University, meeting women, and writing this memoir.

That, dear readers, is the brief overview of my life — now for the fun part!

Mom, Dad, and yours truly. A handsome one year old.

I REMEMBER MAMA

THERE WAS AN old Broadway show, made into a famous movie, called *I Remember Mama*. How well I remember my mother!

Unfortunately, my father died in 1967 before any of my children or my sister Arlene's children were born. Fortunately, my mother lived long enough to meet and to love all three of my children and three (of four) of Arlene's kids. My mother was a loving woman who cared for her children more than anything. She was reserved, protective, and caring, and these traits were inherited by my sister and me.

When I was ten years old, we lived in Brighton Beach, and I was able to go to the beach every afternoon during the summer with my mother and young sister. But first came lunch.

Every day that summer, Mom would make me the same lunch consisting of a hard-boiled egg, and cottage cheese. I was getting tired of this sameness and told my mom that she should make a change. She said okay and the next day she surprised me by serving first the cottage cheese, and then the hard-boiled egg. To this day, I cannot eat hard-boiled eggs!

To say the least, my mom was anything but a baseball fan. One afternoon, I was watching my Dodgers play on our high definition ten-inch television set when Mom asked me to run down to the grocery store. I told her this was an important game, and I must know exactly what's going on. She told me that she would write down everything that was said by the announcer and give it to me when I returned. Her notes were jumbled and the whole situation was really funny, especially the Schaefer beer commercial. I think the Dodgers won that day.

Years later, I was a social young man and often came home very late or better yet, very early in the morning. Sometimes, if I went out during the week, early in the morning, I would meet my father who was getting up to go to work.

One Saturday night, I went out and came home at 2 a.m. My mother heard me come in and got up and asked me if I were sick. "Why do you think that I'm sick?", I asked.

"Because it's 2 o'clock and you always come home at 4 o'clock."

She was right!

I was living at home when I returned from the Army and started my business career. My friends George and Brooks thought it would be a great idea if we could all share an apartment in Manhattan. When I broached the idea to my parents, they were not happy and said, "You'll be a playboy."

What's wrong with that? But, I stayed in Brooklyn!

To subsidize the rent that my parents were paying, I gave them ten dollars each week. I was not a coffee drinker (I still don't drink coffee), but I drank a lot of milk and with my milk, I needed my cookies. One day, I sat down with a gallon of milk and realized there were no cookies to be found. I went to the nearest Waldbaums and filled my shopping cart with every type of cookie imaginable, totaling ten dollars.

My mother was not happy, but my sister was ecstatic!

***

After we were married, Kathy and I, along with her younger sister, Laurie went fishing on a big charter boat out of Sheepshead Bay in Brooklyn. The captain of the boat kept shouting, "You gotta hook 'em before you cook 'em."

I love that line! Actually, we caught quite a few, so we took our haul to my parents apartment which was nearby. No one was home, but I had the key and I stuffed about ten fish into the refrigerator. When my mother returned, she thought that a thief had broken into her apartment but instead of stealing anything, the thief had left her ten fish!

The Brooklyn Police Department could not figure it out.

A few years after my father passed away, my mother remarried. Harry was a nice fellow whose main interest was "What's for dinner?" They moved from Brooklyn to West Palm Beach in 1973, just before Vanessa was born. We came to Florida on Thanksgiving so my mother could meet Vanessa. The meeting went well.

Century Village had a population of about ten thousand senior citizens, and for those who wanted to play tennis, there were two courts. A guest had to play before 8 a.m. and after 5 p.m. but since it got light late and dark early, I was very limited. A friend of my mother's got to the court at 6 a.m. and reserved a court so that I could play at 7 a.m., which was really nice of him. He arranged a game for me with some contemporaries of his — I was 35 and the other players were 85. I brought new tennis balls and one accidentally went on the other court. I called out to the other court, "Excuse me, that Wilson 5 is our ball."

The player on the next court said, "I know that's your ball, Sonny. We play with the same balls every day, and they are so worn that there are no markings on them."

When I finished my terrific game, I left the other players with my new can of balls. They were very appreciative!

***

Three years later, the Karps were coming to Florida to see my mother over the Christmas holidays, and I thought that I would give her a great surprise. I lied and told her that we were not coming this year, but that Jennifer would be coming down with a friend and she would visit her for lunch. We all hid in the bushes as Jennifer knocked on her door. My mom was so happy to see Jennifer, and then five minutes later, Heather knocked on her door. After another five minutes, three-year-old Vanessa knocked on her door. Mom was thrilled!

My mother was not the best cook, but she prepared a roast beef dinner for the family. The meat was very dry and the vegetables were not so great. My kids hated the meal, and not to hurt my mother's feelings, each time she left the room, I took food from someone's plate. Mom was so happy that the kids had empty plates but I was stuffed!

Neil Sedaka's greatest fan was my mother. Neil was a schoolmate of mine and a good friend, and he actually played his first recording on my phonograph for my mother because I was not home. He was giving a concert in Broward County, and I got tickets for everyone. I sent Neil a note before the concert, telling him that my family was in the audience.

He totally surprised everyone when he announced that George Karp was in the audience with his whole family. I was able to go backstage and we all reunited after so many years. My mother could not have been happier!

On New Year's Eve day, I was still playing tennis at 4 o'clock when my mother and Harry came over to say happy new year. They were dressed in formal clothes and I was still dressed in sweaty tennis clothes. I asked what time do people celebrate New Year's in West Palm Beach — 5 p.m.?

My mother said, "Somewhere in the world it's midnight, so happy new year!"

Mom was right again!

In the thirty-seven years since my mom has passed away, she has proven to be prophetic. When I was a teenager, and my mother, being very protective of me, did not approve of one of my friends, she would refer to that boy or that girl as a "TRUMPANIK."

The Yiddish definition of trumpanik is "a blowhard, a boastful person, a braggart, a blower of his own horn," according to *The Joys of Yiddish*.

Do you think that my Democratic mother knew about the election of 2016? I don't think she would categorize Hillary as a "trumpanik."

Yes, I remember Mama!

OH MY PAPA

EDDIE FISHER MADE a hit record in 1953 called "Oh My Papa." The lyrics were written for me singing to my father.

"Oh my Papa, to me he was so wonderful, Oh my Papa, I miss him so today."

My father had many loves. He loved life, he loved his country, he loved his family, and he loved the Brooklyn Dodgers. Although he lacked an extensive education, he truly educated me on many subjects.

In 1946, the Dodgers made history when they signed Jackie Robinson to a contract, integrating baseball for the first time. When I questioned my father about this historic news story, he told me something that I vividly remember, seventy years later. He told me that if Jackie Robinson were to cut his finger, his finger would bleed red blood. He said that if I were to cut my finger, I would also bleed red blood. He got me to realize that whether black or white, all people are created equal. Thomas Jefferson would be proud!

My dad took me to my first baseball game in 1946 when I was seven years old. Ebbets Field looked enormous to me as we sat behind home plate. I studied my scorecard and cheered when the Dodgers came to bat in the first inning. Gil Hodges was up and as I perused my scorecard, I screamed, "Jill, get a hit!"

All around me, everyone was laughing and I didn't know why. My dad explained that his name was pronounced "GIL," not "JILL." My name, George, has a soft G, while his name, Gil, has a hard G. By the fifth inning, I think that I understood.

***

We moved to Brighton 12th Street when I was in the fourth grade. Our home was a small one bedroom apartment with one bathroom. Our family room was the kitchen and we did not have a screening room. I slept in the alcove (when I told this to my kids, they called me "Alky") and I'm still not sure where my sister slept.

A schoolmate of mine Michael invited me to his home, which was a large upscale apartment on the ocean. He had a big terrace and on the terrace was a shuffleboard court. We played and I just loved it. When I got home, I told my parents about the shuffleboard court and asked whether we could get one.

My dad said, "Sure we can get one. We can throw out all of the furniture in the living room, then I'll get a can of paint and I can turn the living room floor into a shuffleboard court!"

I waited a few years, but sadly, it never happened.

***

My fledgling writing career was helped by my father. When I was in the seventh grade, I had to write a composition about my family. I wrote a great story but I could not think of a title. Dad had a great idea and said why don't I call it, "Nothing Fishy about the Karps."

My teacher loved it, the class loved it, and most importantly, I loved it. Dad was so happy that I was happy!

My father was truly a man with a great sense of humor; I wish that I could be as funny as him. We were visiting relatives in the Catskills during the summer of 1952, and my father did a great "shtick." It was very dark that evening and everyone was sitting on the front porch. Dad went into the house, wrapped a white sheet around him and went out the back door. When he came around to the front of the house, he moaned like a ghost and everyone screamed! Two relatives fainted!

My father always made me laugh. One night at dinner, I was eating a bowl of soup. He made me laugh so hard that Campbell's tomato soup came shooting out of my nose! This was strange because I was eating chicken soup.

Dad had nicknames for everyone, mostly disparaging names. My grandmother had a friend Mr. Landau, who had protruding ears. My father nicknamed him "Red Sails" and every time I hear Nat King Cole sing "Red Sails in the Sunset", I think of old Mr. Landau!

There was a barbershop down the block from us, and all of Brighton Beach went there for haircuts. My father nicknamed the barber, "Snotty Sam," which was strange because his name was Irving!

***

To celebrate my graduation from high school, the family went on a July 4th vacation to a hotel in the Catskill Mountains. The hotel was not quite the Concord or Grossingers, but rather a dinky hotel. The festivities for July 4th was a dinner outside and informal entertainment. The hotel owner wanted someone to carry the American flag and picked my father for this job.

My parents had friends who were staying at Kutshers, an upscale resort not far from the downscale hotel where we were staying. My folks were invited to see the show there, and they forced me to go with them. Looking like I was in Gentlemen's Quarterly, I wore a sport jacket and Bermuda shorts with high black socks — the newest style. There was going to be a dance contest and my proud parents insisted that I participate.

With my great outfit, how could I possibly lose. I won a bottle of champagne, but most important, my folks were proud!

Dad let me drive his Buick convertible to school and on dates, and I was pretty cool. I always kept the convertible top down, even on the coldest day. One evening, I forgot to lock the top of the car, and when Dad drove the car the next day on the Belt Parkway, the top flew open and his hat blew off, never to be seen again. He was not a happy camper!

***

In 1962, four years after the Dodgers left Brooklyn, both of us became Mets fans. The Mets were terrible that first year — truly bad, but my father watched every game like it was the World Series. One evening in late September, I was getting ready to go out when I heard my father screaming at the television. I said to him, "Dad, the season is almost over and the Mets are sixty-three games out of first place. Why get excited?"

He knew I was right!

My father, though he was not a philosopher, gave me two bits of scholarly advice. He said, "It's just as easy to fall in love with a rich girl than with a poor girl." Twice, unfortunately, I did not follow his advice.

He also told me, "It's not what you know, but who you know." This bit of advice I do not agree with, unless a person is a Washington lobbyist!

My dad suffered a fatal heart attack in 1967, but right up to the end, he maintained his sense of humor. Just before he died, he whispered to me, "George, look under the garbage can at home for my will and my life insurance policy."

When I got home, I did look but found nothing. With all my sadness, he still made me laugh!

At his funeral I was given a torn black ribbon that I was supposed to wear for a month. After two weeks, I realized that the ribbon was lost and I had to replace it. At that time we lived on Fifth Avenue and 14th Street, and I began to look for a synagogue near our apartment where I could get a new ribbon. Coming home from work, I found a tiny synagogue on East 17th Street and I went in.

I explained to the Rabbi that I needed a new ribbon. The orthodox Rabbi, who was about five feet tall, grabbed me and started to tear the lapel of my brand new suit. I pulled him off me and ran from the building. Now I needed a new ribbon and a new suit!

This is not a funny story but nevertheless the incident is worth telling.

Sadly, Dad never got to see his first grandchild, Jennifer, — named after him — and born three months after he had died. About a year later, I had a strange dream that I could not figure out. In my dream, President Eisenhower was pushing a baby carriage along with his wife, Mamie. What did this mean? — a Democrat like me dreaming about a Republican president. I thought about this dream for many months and then I had an epiphany: The president was really my father and he had a message for me.

"EISENHOWER" really meant "HI SON, HOW ARE YOU."

I was convinced that this was the meaning of the dream and after fifty years, I still remember it vividly.

My father certainly was not a man of means, but what he lacked in his small wallet, he made up for with his big heart. "It isn't what you have but what you are!"

Mom, Dad, Arlene, and the boy wonder, circa 1951.

How about my shirt!

SISTER ACT

MY SISTER ARLENE, though small in size, like our father, is also big in heart!

She has always been there for me — in good times and in bad times. No one has more friends than Arlene, and for good reason. The word BEST, best describes her! She is the best sister, the best wife, the best mother, and the best Nana. I have not had an argument with my sister in probably fifty years!

When she was two years old and I was ten, I taught her the names of all the Brooklyn Dodgers. I took her into the schoolyard and she performed her little tricks:

I would say Jackie, she said Robinson.

I would say Duke, she said Snider.

I would say PeeWee, she said Reese.

Someone told me that I looked like the organ grinder and Arlene was the monkey!

***

Years later, I took her to the beach with me on a sunny June morning. I let her use my sun reflector and she sat there cooking. The next day she was scheduled to have her tonsils removed, and my parents took her to the hospital. When the doctors saw her bright red face, they thought she was having a stroke and they panicked. My mother explained that it was only a sunburn and so, goodbye tonsils!

Arlene and her friends were in the school band. One day she asked me if I could drive her friends and her to school for a concert. The girls were all in full uniform, and I had to put the top down on my dad's old convertible that I was driving. The ten girls sat all over the car and people in the street stared at us. They looked like Sgt. Peppers Lonely Hearts Club Band!

Approaching her sixteenth birthday, Arlene announced that she would be having a sweet-sixteen party at Ben Maksik's, the fanciest nightclub in Brooklyn. I had been there many times in my career, and I knew that this would be a costly party for my parents who could ill afford such an event. But, my mother had saved over the years, and this was something that she wanted to do for her little girl. The party was great!

***

Arlene attended Brooklyn College and there she met Harvey Feldman, whom she would eventually marry. My father, always a great kidder, asked her every day, "How's Hymie?"

Infuriated, Arlene said, "His name is Harvey, not Hymie."

My father responded, "I see. So how's Hymie?"

Fast-forward several years to 1971 and Arlene and Harvey were watching baby Heather for a few days. Heather was not a great sleeper, and I guess I neglected to tell that to them. When we picked up Heather, the Feldman's were relieved. Harvey said, "Heather was a delight, but she got up every night crying at 3 a.m.."

I responded, "That's great, she usually gets up at 2 a.m.!"

***

Arlene is a great cook. Unfortunately, not every dish turns out to be a great dish. One Sunday afternoon, the Karp family traveled to Monroe, New York to visit the Feldmans. Arlene made a clam dip which tasted good and I indulged. Harvey and I went to play tennis at the local indoor tennis club, and I felt the clam dip rumbling around in my stomach, with every backhand that I hit. To say the least, I was gassy and I felt my intestines exploding. I wondered why the tennis players on the next court were holding their noses and running for the exits.

I still play tennis but I never eat clam dip!

Arlene and Harvey now live in Warwick, New York, where Harvey still works (in Monroe) as an optometrist. Their four children and nine grandchildren think that they are the best — so do I!

Arlene and her big brother in Miami — 1953.

Top — Arlene and George 1994.
Bottom — Arlene and Harvey 2017

My favorite photo!
Arlene's Sweet Sixteen Extravaganza at Ben Maksik's
Town and Country Nightclub - 1962.
Arlene, George, Dad and Mom.

THE SUMMER OF LOVE

WHAT CAN A young father feel when his first child is born? Only a feeling, so ecstatic, never to be duplicated in his lifetime. The year 1967 was truly "The Summer of Love!" As we celebrated Israel's unbelievable victory in the Six-day war in 1967, we also celebrated Jennifer's birth.

Three years later, we took Jennifer with us to Puerto Rico. She loved the beach and the ocean, and we all had a great time. Kathy and I went out to dinner one evening and hired the hotel's babysitter. When we returned from dinner, the room was bright and the lady sat on a chair, like a zombie, close to the bed staring at the sleeping Jennifer. When I asked her what she was doing, the sitter replied, "Señor, you told me to watch her, and I am closely watching her."

I could not argue with the sitter!

On Labor Day 1973, the big pool at Mediterranean Towers in Fort Lee, New Jersey, was closing for the season. I wanted Jennifer to jump into the pool and practice her swimming, but she only wanted me to be in the pool to catch her. She stood by the side of the pool, too nervous to jump in. After about an hour, I was starting to turn purple, and she still wouldn't jump. I told her that my hands were getting so wrinkled, I could get a job with SunSweet Prunes. She never jumped!

We had just moved into our new house in Oradell, New Jersey, a big house with a big backyard. To celebrate Jennifer's seventh birthday, we decided to have an outdoor party. The best part was that I had contacted a man who supplied ponies for birthday parties. My daughter invited friends from her old school in Fort Lee, as well as friends from her new school. Lots of kids were coming so I requested three ponies.

The party was a great success and was the social event of the year in Oradell. Fearing that I would have horse manure all over my beautiful backyard, I told the head cowboy to make sure that he gave each pony a large enema before they came to the party!

***

I took Jennifer to a Giants football game at Yankee Stadium along with her uncle Danny. It was a hot day and Danny went to get a soda for Jennifer and a beer for himself. After a while, Jennifer was giggling and singing and I knew something was up. I asked Danny if any of his beer got into Jennifer's orange soda, and he said maybe it had. I took my drunken seven-year-old daughter home and certainly never told her mother!

Being a baseball fan, I tried to convert my children into fans also. I took Jennifer to a Mets game one Saturday afternoon when she was eight. In the first inning, a low flying bird was preparing for a colonoscopy and targeted my new pants. Would you believe that a month later at a Giants football game, possibly the same bird recognized my pants and again went bombs away!

***

Washington's birthday 1976 was going to be a special day for me and my eight-year-old daughter, Jennifer. She had no school, I had no work, and we planned to spend the day together. I had gotten tickets to see the Harlem Globetrotters play that afternoon in Madison Square Garden, and I knew that she would enjoy the game.

That morning we drove to Westchester where I had to see a customer. I finished quickly and Jennifer said to me, "Dad, I'm hungry. Let's have lunch."

I said, "Okay, we can grab a dog at the Garden."

Jennifer got all excited. "Wow! We're getting a dog and I can play with him in our garden. Let's call Mom."

Sadly I had to say, "No, I mean a hot dog that we can eat at Madison Square Garden." She was disappointed but really loved the basketball game.

***

At age sixteen, Jennifer went on a teen tour and really got to see the country. She had given us an itinerary of her trip, so we knew exactly where she was at all times. She called late one night, never realizing the three hour time difference, and I asked her, "Are you enjoying Seattle?"

"Seattle? I'm in San Diego."

She quickly conferred with one of her friends and said, "You're right. Seattle is terrific!"

When she got home from her trip, we were in Westhampton and she was bored. I spoke to the head lifeguard at the Yardarm and asked him if he needed another lifeguard. He said that he did; he knew Jennifer, but she would have to be certified. Being certified as a lifeguard, meant that she would have to rescue a person by towing them in the pool, from one end to the other, several times.

She agreed to do this but needed a person to rescue. Unwillingly, her sister Heather became that person. In the pool, Jennifer grabbed Heather around the neck and attempted to drag her across the pool. This was a comedy of errors as Heather was starting to turn purple in the water, but she was able to rescue Jennifer!

Bottom line, Jennifer did not become a lifeguard!

***

Fast-forward about two years when Jennifer was getting ready to choose a college. We toured the country — Ann Arbor to see Michigan; and Atlanta to see Emory. President Jimmy Carter taught several classes at Emory, and our tour guide showed us his office. The guide told us to wait in his office and we did. Jennifer felt so comfortable that she sat in the president's big chair and started to look through his desk.

"Jennifer, what are you doing? The secret service is outside, and we can be arrested as Russian spies!" I shouted.

Finally, we went to New Orleans to see Tulane, the college that she ultimately chose. We both loved New Orleans, as the food was terrific and the city was just great. We went to the World's Fair of 1984. We were one of the few people to see it since it closed soon thereafter.

Jennifer loved the French Quarter and as we walked through it one evening, I inadvertently stepped in a big batch of New Orleans horse manure! I threw out my shoes and wore bedroom slippers the rest of the trip.

Little Jennifer graduated New York University, Cardozo Law School, and Columbia Graduate School. Not too shabby! She lives with her husband Mark and her son Conrad (a future tennis champion) in Manhattan and Westchester. She still gives me that happy feeling.

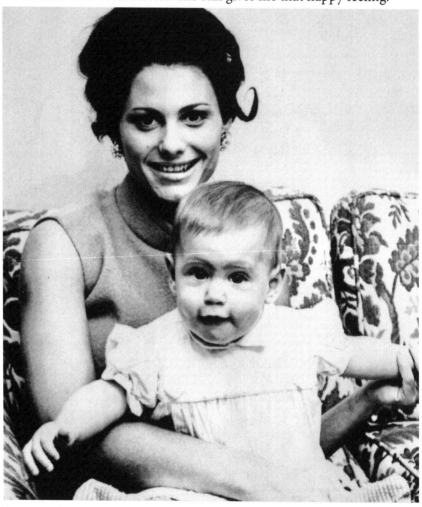

Baby Jennifer with Mama Kathy.
Two pretty ladies!

STAY AS SWEET AS YOU ARE

A T HEATHER'S BAS mitzvah party in April 1983, at Regines, a fancy-shmancy Manhattan club, I did something quite meaningful. Before I made a toast to Heather, I wanted a background song to be played. I gave the bandleader a tape of Nat King Cole singing, " Stay As Sweet As You Are." That song typifies Heather, then and now.

They say that being the middle child is the toughest, but Heather endured. When she was three, we took her and Jennifer to a Japanese hibachi restaurant, Kiku, in Fort Lee. When we got up to leave, I picked her up, over the big table. Accidentally, her foot knocked over a big urn of soy sauce, splattering everyone around the table and drenching me. In a loud voice, Heather said, "My daddy did it, my daddy did it!"

I apologized to everyone around the table, but I didn't say, "Heather did it, Heather did it!"

***

Heather was not a baseball enthusiast, but Kathy enrolled her in Little League when she was eight. Kathy also enrolled me as the coach of the team, of course without my knowledge. Heather liked Little League, but I loved it! She was not as good as the boys on the team and she was the only girl. She needed help and I was the helper.

Twice a week, before games, I would come home early and work on her swing. We had a big backyard in Oradell, and I used a big bucket of tennis balls, softly pitching to the Little League's Reggie Jackson. Heather finally got the hang of it, and she was hitting balls all over the backyard. When the games finally started, Heather played and she actually got a couple of hits!

Both of us retired after season one!

***

Six years later, Heather was still not a baseball fan, but was delighted to accompany me in going to the baseball Hall of Fame in Cooperstown, New York. Both of us really enjoyed that weekend, seeing all the photos, plaques, movies, and especially the blueberry muffins. Babe Ruth became Heather's hero!

That summer, we went to Tanglewood in the Berkshires for a few days. I got tickets for a night concert under the stars that was terrific, except the grass was wet. Heather borrowed a canvas beach chair from some people sitting nearby, but she must have eaten too much for dinner because as she sat on the chair, the whole thing broke. She was embarrassed and did not want to return the broken chair, but I convinced her that she had to face the music. Reluctantly, she apologized to the people who did not seem to care about the chair. Heather felt much better and I think she learned two valuable lessons — face the music and don't eat too much!

***

When Heather graduated from NYU in 1992, I had made the decision to move to Boca Raton. I asked her if she would like to drive with me to Florida and help me in moving. She agreed and we made the long journey, stopping in Williamsburg (not the one in Brooklyn), Charleston, and Savannah. Trying to catch the ferry in Cape May, New Jersey, Heather got caught speeding, and I could not talk her way out of the ticket.

We stopped at a restaurant in South Carolina where they had a buffet featuring barbecue. I asked the waitress, "What kind of barbecue is this, — beef, pork, or chicken?"

She said, "Man, I don't know, it's just barbecue! Where are you from anyway?"

When I told her I was from Iowa, I think she understood.

Heather was a great help in getting me organized in Florida. A short time later, she decided to move in with me in my nice apartment in

Boca. But realizing that she was a New York girl and not a Boca girl, six months later she moved back to New York. We had a tearful goodbye at the airport, and I knew just how much I would miss her!

***

About twenty years later, now married with children, Heather decided to pay the old man a weekend visit. At the airport waiting for them, I noticed a young woman dressed in a costume. The woman was wearing a Bullwinkle costume, and she was waiting for a friend. I started a conversation and told her that I was waiting for my grandchildren who would really enjoy seeing me with Bullwinkle. She agreed to stand with me and when the kids arrived, she put on Bullwinkle's head and put her arm around me. Heather and her kids thought that this was the greatest!

***

One morning, when Heather was six, she had a bagel with cream cheese for breakfast. On the bus, going to her day camp, she felt sick and proceeded to throw up all over everything. She decided that cream cheese was the culprit and she has not eaten any cream cheese for the past forty years. I told her that she was putting the Breakstone Company out of business!

At her fortieth birthday party, I gave her a wrapped present of a bar of Philadelphia Cream Cheese. Heather laughed but did not eat it! How's that for holding a grudge!

She now lives in New Jersey with her husband Jordan and their wonderful children, Elizabeth and Evan, who do eat cream cheese! My daughter Heather has absolutely lived up to the title of the song, "Stay As Sweet As You Are!"

Three year old Heather at her birthday party.
Definitely not a cream cheese cake!

VANESSA IS A JOY

I DON'T KNOW IF any name fits a person any better than the name of my third and youngest daughter, Vanessa Joy. When we traveled to London and Paris in 1985, Vanessa refused to go into any of the French or English churches. She cried and said, "If I go into a church, then I won't be Jewish anymore."

We would have to change her name to Vanessa GOY!

When she was born, I had grown a mustache. The next winter, Kathy and I were going to Acapulco, and to get the most sun on my pale face, I shaved off my mustache. When one-year-old Vanessa saw me without the mustache, she thought I was a stranger, and she wouldn't stop crying. After five years, she finally got over it!

For many years, I had a regular tennis game on Sunday mornings. Driving home, I would stop at the bagel store and buy bagels and nova for the family's breakfast. Wearing my tennis outfit, I would come home to deliver the breakfast goodies. One evening, when Vanessa was two, I got dressed to play tennis. When she saw my tennis outfit, she asked, "Where are the bagels?"

Pavlov and his dogs would have been impressed with that experiment!

To celebrate Jennifer's bas mitzvah in 1980, our family went to Israel with a group of Oradell neighbors. On our first bus ride, the tour guide wanted everyone to introduce themselves, so the microphone was passed around the bus. Now a few weeks before the trip, I had taken the family to see the Broadway show, *Annie*. Redheaded Vanessa was convinced that she was the redheaded *Annie*. Back in the bus, when

Vanessa got the microphone, I said to her, "Why don't you sing one of the songs from *Annie*?"

She burst into "Tomorrow, Tomorrow, I'll Love You Tomorrow", and got a resounding ovation. She loved it!

When we came to Florida in 1982, we were driving on I95 one day, and Vanessa noticed a sign. She said, "Look, Dad. It says Boynton Beach. Didn't you grow up in Boynton Beach?"

"Close," I replied. "How about Brighton Beach, only a thousand miles apart!"

When Vanessa was ten, one Saturday afternoon, father and daughter went out for lunch. Did she want pizza or hot dogs or Chinese food — the choice was hers. We were driving around looking for a restaurant when I saw "Sizzlers." I drove into the parking lot and Vanessa said that she didn't want to eat there. I said why not and she replied, "I don't like the cars parked there!"

I took her for a hot dog next door to the Mercedes dealer and she was happy!

***

I retired from my business in 1984 and I had the best time. I really got to spend a lot of time with my kids and we all loved it. Vanessa was in a school play, *Tom Sawyer*, and I was the only father in the audience — and a proud one. She appreciated that!

Vanessa loved dogs and I loved the idea of not having a dog. Kathy met a woman who knew a dog breeder in New Jersey, and one day Kathy and the girls drove to see the breeder's dogs. Vanessa called me from New Jersey and begged me to allow her to get the cutest little white puppy. I said, "For fifty years, I've gotten along without a dog. I don't need one and I don't want one!"

She begged and begged and because I've never said "no" to any of my children, Pebbles soon became a member of the family.

Vanessa, now living in California, has three dogs. Her husband, Darryl and her children, Stella and Jeremy love all their little dogs.

Vanessa is truly a joy!

Big sister Jennifer holding Vanessa — 1974.

GRANDPARENT'S DAY

EVEN THOUGH I was very young, I still have memories of my grandparents, my mother's mother and father. They were old European people, from Austria, who never really assimilated to the American way. I think that even when they were young, they were old!

My grandmother was a good cook. Her specialty was stewed fruit — very useful for a person preparing for a colonoscopy!

Granny had difficulty with her pronunciation — she pronounced the word "vegetable," vegeTABLE. Whenever she said it, I was always looking under the table for something!

She used the word "DESSN'T" to mean DON'T. "Georgilla, you dessn't go out in the street."

I used the word dessn't in my College application to Harvard — they dessn't accept me!

I remember that my grandfather would always give me prunes to eat. He said that since I'm three years old, I can have three prunes. Now that I'm a bit older, I can eat seventy-eight prunes.

When I do, I spend most of my day in the bathroom! Thanks, Grandpa!

THE NEW NEIGHBORHOOD

M Y PRE-BRIGHTON BEACH life had me growing up in nearby Sheepshead Bay. I lived on East 19th Street between Avenue Y and Avenue Z. On Avenue Y, stood P.S. 254, the public elementary school. On Avenue Z, stood St. Mark's Church school, a private Catholic school. P.S. 254 was known as the Jewish school; while St. Mark's was known as the Catholic school. Of course, I went to the Jewish school; Catholics in the neighborhood went to St. Mark's. I guess Protestant kids were lucky as they didn't have to go to school at all!

We lived in a nice private house where the owners, a lovely Nazi couple, lived in the basement. My father, always quick with a nickname, dubbed the landlady, "The Witch."

My sister Arlene was born there, and since the Nazi couple did not supply too much heat for their Jewish tenants, my parents decided to move.

My mother was very protective of me, so I was not a very outgoing child. In Sheepshead Bay, I only had a few friends and they lived a few blocks away. All this changed when we moved to Brighton Beach. Our apartment building was just across the street from P.S. 225, which had a giant schoolyard. On Saturday, my first day there, I went into the schoolyard and couldn't believe what I saw. There were literally hundreds of kids playing softball, basketball, and football all in the same schoolyard, all at the same time! Softball players were running into basketball players who were running into football players!

My father had an idea for me that would ingratiate me with the schoolyard kids. I liked hockey; the New York Rangers were my favorite team. For my eighth birthday that year, Dad bought me an official blue Rangers' jersey that I just loved. He told me to wear the jersey whenever I went into the schoolyard. He told me that when kids would come over to me and ask how I got the jersey, I would have to tell a little lie.

In those days, almost all professional hockey players were Canadian. There was one American who played for the Rangers, and he was a tough defenseman named Bill Moe. My dad told me that when asked, I should say, "Bill Moe gave me this jersey. Uncle Bill is married to my aunt."

I told this story many times and I think I started to believe it myself. Now everyone in the schoolyard knew me and they called me "Bill Moe." I kept the jersey all these years, and finally, since my grandson Jeremy was a hockey fan, I gave the jersey to him. My daughter Vanessa had it framed, and it now resides proudly in Los Angeles, on Jeremy's bedroom wall!

***

In the basement of our apartment house, there was one washing machine that all forty-eight tenants in the building shared. My cousin Sidney, who lived in the building, was a devious guy. He was able to drill a hole into a dime, attach a string to it, and slip it into the coin slot, thus starting the machine. Just once, he let me use it, but I felt very guilty doing it and never asked for the dime on the string again.

One of my chores was to bring clothes to the basement and do the wash. Mom told me to use only a little detergent, but of course I didn't listen to her. I liked to use a lot of detergent and flood the machine with soapsuds. I got so good at this that I was able to flood the room. Many complaints came to my mother about her juvenile delinquent son flooding the basement with soapsuds!

Besides being devious, cousin Sidney was a bully. There was a big blizzard over Christmas that year, 1947, and the snow was piled high. I was outside playing in the snow and Sid told some of the kids in the building to rough me up. They did and really beat me up. That night, at Sid's urging, about ten of these kids came to my apartment with games to apologize to me.

I really felt good now — I knew that I was one of the Brighton Boys!

MY OLDEST FRIEND

WHAT CAN YOU say about a friendship that is seventy years old?

The Karp family moved to Brighton 12th Street in 1947, and the first person that I met was my new friend Mel. We were both the same age and immediately bonded. My sister Arlene became best friends with his sister Sharon, while my parents became good friends with his folks. We lived in apartment 4D and they lived in apartment 2D, and when the windows were open, since they were not quiet people, we overheard every one of their conversations and arguments. Mostly, there were arguments and they would scream!

Mel was a terrific ballplayer, often playing with kids five years older than him. He batted left-handed, and when we played stickball in the inner schoolyard, he killed my pitching. To compensate, he batted right-handed and then did even better against my pitching.

He resembled a television star of that era — Howdy Doody! But whenever someone called him "Howdy," instead of being insulted, he just laughed.

In those early years, we collected baseball cards. Playing poker for baseball cards was a big thing in the schoolyard. We arranged a poker game with some younger kids on the next block, and Mel was the dealer and I was a player across from him. I don't know how he did it, but I always got the best cards, and since we were partners, we went home with hundreds of baseball cards. We were not invited back!

Mel was always getting into trouble, always being chased across the schoolyard by someone, usually older, bigger, and slower!

There was a luncheonette on Brighton Beach Avenue, in business for a long time, that was owned by several brothers. The store was nicknamed the "40 Thieves." When Mel was about twelve, he bought a newspaper and said to one of the brothers, "You must be one of the Thieves." The brother became infuriated and chased Mel all the way down Brighton Beach Avenue, but never caught him!

When we were both about fifteen, we got jobs as bus boys in the cafeteria of Brighton Beach Baths, a terrible job. Another busboy dared Mel to do something ridiculous, like peeing in the big coffee urn. Mel took his dare, and bottom-line, all the old "yentas" loved the coffee that day!

***

A couple of years later, several of us were invited by a few girls to go on a television dance program, the "Herb Sheldon Show." This was the 1950s, sixty years before HBO and Netflix. The television station was waiting to broadcast something important from the United Nations, that was supposed to happen any minute. Until the UN vote was ready, they kept the Herb Sheldon show on indefinitely. The fifteen-minute show lasted about three hours, and we all danced and danced. To say the least, we hogged the camera, with Mel being the biggest hog!

Finally, the show ended and the producer asked us to come into his office. I thought that he was so impressed with our dancing he would ask us to be regulars on the show. I was wrong! Angrily, he said, "If I ever see any of you again on my program, I'll throw you out on your Brooklyn asses!"

That ended our television careers!

***

A few years earlier, as a sophomore in high school, I tried out unsuccessfully for the basketball team. The coach informed me, assessing my basketball ability, that I should try out for the ping pong team. However, he did offer me the job as water boy!

Then at twenty, I met a very nice girl, Margie. On our first date, I rang her bell and who answered the door — her father, the Lincoln basketball coach who ended my basketball career. He had no idea who I was, but I reminded him, and he apologized.

I made plans to double date with Mel and his girlfriend, Eileen, whom he later married. They wanted to go to a driving range to hit golf balls and I agreed. Margie was a golfer but the three of us were not. My friend Mel, the athlete, had never played golf and was having a hard time. Margie started to show me what I was doing wrong and corrected my swing. Miraculously, I started to hit long and straight while Mel was hitting ground balls to third base. This was the first time that I had ever surpassed Mel in any sport and I was thrilled!

Every time that I mention this story to Mel, he says he doesn't remember. A likely story!

***

Mel's father Charlie was a tough old guy and the two never really got along, especially in later years. Even though Mel and I were the same age, he regarded me as his father.

Besides being an athlete, Mel was a great student, eventually becoming a PhD. He lives in Los Angeles and is a professor at UCLA. We see each other when I visit my daughter Vanessa, and even though we haven't seen each other for a year or two or three, it's like we had seen each other the week before. There's something about childhood friends that you just can't replace!

My oldest friend Mel (right) and I at my grandson Jeremy's bar
mitzvah in 2017.

STRIKE THE BELL

THE APARTMENT BUILDING that I lived in on Brighton 12th Street was a pre-war building — not pre-World War II but pre-World War I!

It was very dark and dreary, kind of dirty, but to me it was home. The building had a slow-moving elevator that frequently got stuck. One day, at age ten, I was in the elevator with a neighbor, Mrs. Rothstein, who came from London. In her dignified English accent, she said to me, "Young man, can you please strike the bell."

Not knowing what she meant, I stared at her, blankly. She repeated, "Please strike the bell."

I told her that I didn't know what she was saying. Finally she shrieked, "Push the God damn button!"

Now, she was speaking my language!

THE BLIND MAN

ONE EVENING, WHEN I was about ten years old, at the dinner table, I told my folks that I had an unbelievable story to tell.

"I just can't believe it," I said. "How can a person who cannot see be able to drive a car? It's impossible."

Mom and Dad listened as I told them that I had seen a truck that day, that in big letters on the side of the truck read *A BLIND MAN DRIVES THIS TRUCK.* My parents both started to laugh and my father explained, "Yes, the driver was a blind man. But, he sold Venetian blinds and he really could see."

I got the concept and after sixty-five years, I still think it's funny.

THE BUBBLEGUM THIEF

S A TEN year old, going to the Oceana Theater every week was a treat. Besides the two feature films that were shown, there was a cartoon, news of the week, a serial, and coming attractions. For twenty-five cents, this was a huge bargain. But the best part of going to the movies, was buying and eating candy. Five cent Raisinets and Goobers were among my favorites because it took a long while to finish the box. However, the best time killer for a four hour show was Bonomo's Turkish Taffy, which was subsidized by a local dentist!

Everyone bought their goodies at Nat's, a small candy store next to the theater. Some of my ten-year-old friends had a new hobby — stealing. I had never stolen anything in my short life, but one day, before going to the movies, I reached for a piece of Tattoo bubble gum in Nat's.

Out of nowhere, Mrs. Nat appeared and grabbed my hand. I don't know how she knew that I was going to pocket the bubblegum; maybe I was talking to myself and I was discussing the dastardly act. I think that this misadventure influenced the rest of my life, leading me to live honestly, morally, and with great integrity! Also, never to have a tattoo!

The gum cost one penny and for the penny, she threatened to tell my mother.

Can you imagine if she caught me stealing a Tootsie Roll for five cents?

Would she call my grandmother?

MY TERRIBLE MISTAKE

A S AN ELEVEN year old, I thought that my cousin Bert had the best job in the world. He sold peanuts at Ebbets Field, home of the Brooklyn Dodgers. He got to know many of the players on the team, and one day, Bert asked a favor of Jackie Robinson. Bert gave Jackie a new baseball and asked him if everyone on the team could sign the ball. Jackie complied and gave Bert the ball signed by Snider, Hodges, Campanella, and everyone else on the Dodgers.

Bert came to visit us one day and gave me an early birthday present — the signed baseball! I was so happy with the ball that I even slept with it for a while.

Then I made a terrible, terrible mistake. I took the ball downstairs to the schoolyard across the street, to show it off to my new friends. Everybody was really impressed but then one of the boys asked if we could have a catch with the ball. I said sure, but don't let it hit the ground because then it would get scuffed. Of course, the ball hit the concrete and quickly became scuffed. Soon, the autographs were gone and soon the ball was gone. At the end of the day, all I had left was a pile of string from what used to be a baseball.

Can you imagine what the value of an autographed baseball of the 1950 Brooklyn Dodgers would be worth today? Probably a lot more than the pile of string that I still have!

WHAT IF / A PARALLEL UNIVERSE

THIS IS A story that I had written a few years ago. I submitted it to The *New York Times, The Wall Street Journal* and a few other publications, but I guess it was too good to publish! Actually, it appeared in The *Jewish Journal.*

My story:

In 1901, a sixteen-year-old Jewish girl from Hungary, Kati Berger, along with several brothers and sisters, arrived at Ellis Island in New York. A brother and sister who remained in Europe, eventually both perished in a Nazi death camp in 1942. Young Kati settled in Mount Vernon, New York, and subsequently met and married a young trolley car conductor, a devout Catholic from Italy, John Branca. The Brancas ultimately became the proud parents of sixteen children, but Kati secretly kept her Jewish heritage to herself, never telling her children that by Jewish law, they indeed were Jewish. Their children all grew up to be observant Catholics.

A son, Ralph, born in 1926, grew to be a great athlete and in 1943, signed a major league baseball contract to pitch for the Brooklyn Dodgers. Ralph won twenty-one games for the Dodgers in 1947 and was selected for three All-Star games.

In 1951, Ralph went from being famous to infamous, because of one pitch that he threw. That year, the Dodgers and the New York Giants finished the season tied for first place, with identical records, and so a three game playoff was scheduled to determine who would play the New York Yankees in the World Series. On Monday, October 1, Ralph Branca started and lost game one. Game two saw Brooklyn win big, and so game three would determine who would win the National League title.

In one of the greatest baseball games ever played, the Dodgers held a 4-1 lead in the bottom of the ninth inning. Don Newcombe the Dodger ace, pitched brilliantly but became exhausted, giving up a run with two runners on base, when the Dodger manager elected to go to the bullpen. Ralph Branca was brought in to relieve Newcombe, and to face the Giants' Bobby Thomson.

On Branca's second pitch, Thomson hit the "shot heard round the world," a three run homer that won the game, won the pennant, and broke the heart of Brooklyn! Branca was traumatized and at age twenty-five, his once stellar career was basically over.

What's the point of retelling a baseball story that has been rehashed for over sixty years? Well, what if Kati had told her children that indeed she was Jewish and what if her children grew up as observant Jews? The point is that Rosh Hashonah, the Jewish New Year, started at sundown on Sunday, September 30 and into Monday, October 1. What if Ralph Branca, as an observant Jew, said he would not pitch the first playoff game on Monday. The Dodgers had a deep pitching staff and certainly another pitcher had a strong chance of winning game one.

Since they easily won game two, then game three would not have been necessary. Bobby Thomson would not be famous, and Ralph Branca would not be infamous.

What if Kati had served blintzes, borscht, and bagels, instead of canoli, cacciatore, and calzone — then the Dodgers might have won the pennant and might have finally won the World Series!

TALES OF THE SUBWAY

MANY PEOPLE THINK of Subway as only a place to eat, but to New Yorkers the subway is the best way to travel.

In June 1952, my father came home from work with a great story to tell me. He said, "You would not believe who I was talking to on the subway today. Three Cincinnati Reds players asked me directions to get to Ebbets Field. We had a nice talk and I told them that the Dodgers were going to kill them tonight. The Reds' players all laughed and said that's not going to happen!"

Dad and I watched the game on our large-screen ten inch TV and we could not believe that the Dodgers scored **fifteen runs** in the first inning, setting a new MLB record. The Reds must have had red faces that night!

Years later, I took the subway to CCNY downtown when I transferred schools in my junior year of college. I was taking a class in Political Science and one of my assignments was to read the *Daily Worker*. This newspaper was a Communist publication but because we live in a free society, anyone could buy it and read it. Brighton Beach was a hotbed of socialism so there were many smiling faces when I was seen reading the paper. When other people got on the train at the next stop, they were not too happy to sit next to a young Communist!

I did my homework on the subway in the morning because I usually was out on the town the night before. Finals were approaching and I was studying on the train. That night at dinner, I told my parents that I had a big test the next day, and I would be up all night studying.

As soon as I said that, I got a mysterious phone call from a young lady who told me that she had seen me on the train that morning and she wanted to meet me. I told her that I was studying for finals, but she told me that her parents were away, and she really wanted to meet me. I put two and two together, jumped in the shower, and told my folks that I would be studying with a classmate. I doubt that they believed this story, but their little boy could never do any wrong.

I went to the mystery girl's house in Manhattan Beach and she was right, her parents were not home. What she did not tell me, was that her big brother was home and he was not too happy to see me. He asked me, "Would you like to see my pet?"

And I answered, "Of course, I love dogs and cats (I lied)."

He came into the room with a huge cat, an Ocelet, which resembled a leopard! The forty pound cat was on a thick chain and to say the least, I was nervous.

I ran all the way home!

I WAS NOT THE NATURAL

I TRIED AS HARD as I could, but I would never be a good ballplayer. Unlike Robert Redford, I was not *THE NATURAL*. For a young person, being a good athlete was the most important thing. In my mind, I think that I disappointed my father, who in his youth, was a semipro baseball player. I disappointed myself, but I sublimated and became a good student.

I practiced playing basketball many hours during the week, from the time I was ten until I was about fifteen. Living across the street from my school, I played all day Saturday and Sunday and three nights during the week. Evaluating my game, I can say that I couldn't jump, I wasn't a very good shot, I wasn't very fast, and I wasn't a good defender. Other than that, I was a pretty good basketball player!

My mother was not very strict with me, but she did give me one edict. For one month before my bar mitzvah, I was not allowed to play basketball for fear that I would get hurt. The boys in the schoolyard were not losing their best player! Actually, I did get hurt playing basketball a few months later. I got hit in the eye and I thought I was blind. My mom took me to an eye doctor in Brighton, who told her it wasn't serious and gave me an eye patch to wear. Everyone in school thought that I was a cool cat with my patch.

I was hanging around the schoolyard one afternoon, and I was asked to umpire a softball game. One of the biggest and best players was named "Brother," and he definitely was not my brother. I was umpiring behind the pitcher, Brother was up, and he hit a line drive that hit me almost in the area "where the sun don't shine." A couple of inches lower and there would be no children and no grandchildren to read my book!

One evening, I was involved in a full-court basketball game at Night Center at P.S. 225. We didn't have uniforms and I was wearing a T-shirt and a bathing suit. While we were playing, a joker on the other team, Larry, pulled down my bathing suit. I didn't know whether to pull up my bathing suit or to go up for a rebound. Needless to say, I was embarrassed!

I joined a local facility, the Shorefront Jewish Center, which organized games against other local Centers. Boxscores of all these local games were carried in the famous Brooklyn newspaper, *The Brooklyn Eagle.* The highlight of my basketball career occurred when I scored seven points in one of these games. I couldn't wait to see the morning's edition of *The Eagle* and much to my dismay, they spelled my name KAYS. There went my basketball career!

When the warm weather came, we played softball in the schoolyard. Evaluating my game, I wasn't a good hitter, I wasn't a good fielder, and my throwing was erratic. Other than that, I wasn't bad! Again, similar to my basketball prowess!

One Sunday morning, when I was a senior in high school, a softball game was arranged between my fraternity and a group of older guys, who were in college. My father, who was always in the schoolyard, was umpiring this game. It was the last inning and my team was losing by one run. Two men were on base for us, there were two out and guess who was up? Two strikes were on me and then I swung and I hit the ball off the centerfield fence. Both runners scored, we won the game, and I was the hero!

I was so happy, but not as happy as my proud father!

***

Years later, Kathy and I were visiting my cousin Bob and his family at a hotel in the Catskills. That afternoon, some of the men started to play softball, and I was asked to play.

I hadn't played in ten years, but I figured that I was safe because I was in my twenties and the other players were in their fifties. Since there was nothing else to do at the hotel, there was a big audience watching the game. I was up and even though I hadn't swung a bat in years, I swung and hit a very long foul ball to right field. I think I struck out but that was irrelevant. At the end of the inning, a man approached me and asked, "Excuse me, but are you a professional baseball player?"

I loved it! After that question, I formally retired from baseball, awaiting my election to the Hall of Fame!

DRIVING TO MIAMI

SINCE THE EIGHTH grade at P.S. 225, Brooks has been my very good friend. All through high school, college, and certainly the single years before marriage, Brooks and I had a special relationship. We were both social people and enjoyed going places, not Europe or Asia, but more like Westhampton, Fire Island, the Concord, and Dubrows. Most of our memorable stories took place when we both were in our early 20's.

A friend of mine told me that there were plenty of great looking girls at the beach clubs on Long Island. In particular, he told me that the Lido Beach Club was a great place to go, but it was a private club. However, he gave me the best information and told me that it was possible to sneak in, by just walking through the kitchen.

Brooks and I drove to Long Island one sunny Sunday, and both of us walked through the kitchen, into the club. We met lots of bikini-clad girls, took plenty of phone numbers, and had the best time. The next Sunday was a repeat of the past Sunday. The third Sunday was a little bit different. I was walking around, drink in hand, like a regular member. A well-dressed man started a conversation with me and asked me if I were a new member. "Not really," I replied, "I'm a personal friend of Mr. Sunshine, the owner of the club, who invited me today."

The man angrily looked at me and said, "I'm Mr. Sunshine. Get the hell out of here and never come back!"

The next Sunday, we stayed in Brighton Beach!

***

Just after I started to work for my cousin Bob, Brooks and I decided to go to Florida over Washington's Birthday weekend. Brooks' grandmother lived in Miami Beach, and although it wasn't the Eden Roc, the price was right. Brooks had his own car, a Ford convertible, and we decided to drive down to sunny Florida. Our mothers packed sandwiches for us, and we hit the road at 4 a.m. We took turns driving and it was an endless day. Finally, at 10 p.m. in Statesboro, Georgia, it was my turn to drive. I couldn't see straight and I gave the keys to Brooks. He told me that it was my turn to drive, but I said, "I can't drive anymore, besides, it's your car."

He took the keys and drove away, leaving me alone in Statesboro, Georgia. I considered going to the Jewish Center, but I heard that they were having a Ku Klux Klan meeting that night. He came back in ten minutes, laughing!

The next day, getting close to Miami, we stopped at Vero Beach, the spring training home of the Los Angeles Dodgers. I couldn't believe it, but because it was a holiday, there was no spring training that day. We walked around and came upon a group of ten-year-olds. I said to Brooks, "Call me Duke (Snider) and I'll call you Sandy (Koufax)."

The kids asked us for autographs and, of course, we signed!

Finally, we reached grandma's house, and she couldn't have been nicer. She made me scrambled eggs each morning and honestly, every time I have scrambled eggs now, I think of Brooks' grandmother. I don't think that she is still alive. After all, she would be about 135 years old!

We hung out at the Fontainebleau Hotel, day and night, met plenty of nice looking girls and had the best time. I sat with my sun reflector and got a terrific sunburn, that my dermatologist now thanks me for!

***

That year, we went skiing over the Christmas holiday to the Berkshires in Massachusetts. Thank goodness, it was so cold that they closed the slopes — so no skiing. That certainly was okay with me because I didn't know the first thing about skiing, and I hated cold weather. Brooks said that we saw more ice in our drinks than we did on the slopes!

Not funny, but Brooks and I had a near-death experience one Sunday night. We had dates with two girls from Manhattan and coming home, discussing our exploits, a car in the entrance to the Brooklyn Battery Tunnel, was going the wrong way. Coming around a curve, he was in the left lane going eighty miles per hour, and we were luckily in the right lane. I was shaking for a week!

Brooks and I had a special code that we used on Saturday nights. If we went out on a double date that was ending early, I would say to him, "You're quite the elegant one tonight."

What that meant was, "Do you want to go to the Club Elegante tonight at 1 a.m.?"

Brooks was always there!

The night at the Carlisle Hotel that I met Kathy, Brooks was there. He was an usher at my wedding, and when he got married, I ushered at his wedding.

One evening, in October 1986, a group of us had dinner at Harvey's house, watching the Mets in the World Series. My old friends, Harvey, Brooks, George, and Hank were all having the best of times. Harvey, Hank, and George R. are all gone now and I miss them very much.

I remember saying to Brooks that night, "You know, I think that one old friend is worth ten new friends."

How right I was!

TOP — Harvey, skinny me, Al, and Brooks — 1957.

BOTTOM - Brooks, yours truly, and George R. — 2008.

BRIGHTON'S BRIGHTEST STAR

NEIL SEDAKA WAS destined to be a star!

In the eighth grade, everyone knew this but nobody, including Neil himself, could ever imagine that he would be such a star. Neil was a great classical pianist and he performed at every show in the P.S. 225 auditorium. He was my friend and after school, when I went to practice basketball, Neil would practice piano. I guess he made the right choice.

In high school, in 1954, Neil started to fool around with a new type of music — Rock 'n Roll. He formed a vocal group, the Tokens, which included my friends Hank and Jay. Neil wrote a few songs that were recorded by others, and he was starting to make a name for himself. My mother was Neil's greatest fan!

Just before graduation from Lincoln, all of my friends were at Bay 3, the public beach in Brighton. We got caught in a huge thunderstorm, and Neil invited everyone to his apartment, just down the block. Neil's mother knew that I was sick recently with pleurisy and she insisted that I change my clothes and take a hot shower. How many people have taken a shower in Neil Sedaka's bathtub!

By the late 1950s, Neil was one of the biggest stars in the record industry. Songs that he wrote and recorded became huge hits — "Oh, Carol," "Breaking Up Is Hard To Do," "Calendar Girl," etc.

In 1982, Neil's wife invited me to a big party celebrating his twenty-five years in show business. The party was terrific and it was great seeing Neil and so many old friends. Neil performed at the Kravis Center in West Palm Beach around 2005 and I got tickets. I was able to go backstage after the show and Neil was so very happy to see me and to meet my wife, Rita. There were many hugs!

***

In 1982, Neil wrote his autobiography, "Laughter in the Rain." I quote from page 42:

"One day my cousin Marlene Hoffman, one of the Brighton 13th St. gang, heard me play my songs. As a result, miracle of miracles, I was invited to my first teenage party. Most of the popular kids in the neighborhood were attending, including "perfect" George Karp and Hank Medress, who became a member of the group I later founded, The Tokens. Everyone seemed to love my songs, and I really knew I had arrived when the girls turned their eyes from George Karp to listen to me for a few minutes."

Everyone was right — Neil had become a star!

Neil, George, and Howdy Doody — 1954.

THE OTHER GEORGE

HAVING A FRIEND is good; having a best friend is great! Of all the many friends that I have had over the years, my best friend was George R — the other George. What makes a best friend? Someone who is compassionate, supportive, thoughtful, reliable, empathetic, trusting, and one who laughs at your jokes.

For the most part, George had these qualities.

When I first met George, he was a curly-haired, chubby boy who turned into a bald, skinny man! He lived in a beautiful apartment building (for Brighton Beach) and I always teased him that he was rich because he had a big electric fan in his apartment. What I first remember about George was that he always wore to school a yellow shirt jacket (a cubavera) that had his name monogrammed on it. I hoped that he would lose it and I would find it!

Many years later, he had a party to celebrate his sixtieth birthday. I wanted to get him something special, so I went to the Gap and bought him a bright yellow knit shirt, the same ugly color of his shirt jacket. Then I found an embroiderer who monogrammed GEORGE on the shirt. George loved the present!

George pledged for my high school fraternity (I was already a member), and I really worked him over. One Sunday, I told him to call me at 6 p.m. exactly. He was out with his parents at Lundy's, a wonderful restaurant that I would go to every five years or so. Cell phones were unknown, so he called me from a phone booth. "Pledge, are you on your knees when you are talking to me?", I demanded.

I heard a lot of noise and commotion from the phone both and then he said, "Yes, I am, Sir."

His father, standing next to the phone booth, thought that he was nuts!

When we were seniors in high school, George was invited by Judy, a popular girl, to go on a boat ride on a Sunday. For some reason, she invited me to be her escort to her friend's sweet sixteen party on the Saturday night before the boat ride. The party, at the best nightclub in Brooklyn, Ben Maksiks, had as its featured performer, a fantastic young singer, Harry Belafonte.

I can't blame George for being perturbed — he got a boat ride on a rainy Sunday (I heard he was sea sick), and I got to see Harry Belafonte!

The other George was not a terrific athlete except for the one sport that he excelled at — ping pong! Late one night, I drove George to our frat house, where we had just installed a new ping pong table. We started to play and my friend won the first game easily, as well as the second game, etc. After winning the first ten games, he said he was bored and wanted to go home. "Oh, no," I said, "not until I beat you." Finally, after about another five games, I won! I think that he was playing with his eyes closed.

*****

On New Year's Eve, 1959, we took our dates to a party, eventually took them home, and then we all went to Dubrows cafeteria, to lie about our exploits. About 4 a.m., George, Brooks, and I made a connection with three girls, and since my parents were away in Florida, we all decided to have a predawn party in my apartment. Everything was going well when at 5 a.m. the phone rang — it was George's father, looking for his twenty-year old little boy.

George sprinted home, down Brighton 12th Street, looking like an Olympic runner. He ruined the party!

George had a girlfriend Ellen, who introduced me to her best friend Marion. Both girls went to a college near Syracuse — Cazenovia. My friend Brooks, was also dating a girl from Cazenovia and the three of us flew to Syracuse for a special college weekend. There were not many hotels in the area, so the girls made plans for us to stay in a doctor's house, which was about two hundred years old. I slept in the doctor's examination room, where my roommate was a skeleton, watching over me from a corner of the room. I didn't sleep too well that night!

The next evening, the girls invited us to the big dance. Brooks, always thinking, brought his attaché case to the dance, which contained bottles of vodka, gin, scotch, and bourbon. Since alcohol was forbidden at the dance, we had to be very secretive with his cache. Unfortunately, we were caught and the girls got into big trouble with the school. All that we could do was apologize.

Sunday morning, our flight was canceled because there was about thirty inches of snow on the ground. We had to stand on the train home for about six hours. That was the last time I saw Syracuse!

***

One summer night in 1962, George and I took our dates to a beach club on Long Island. The show's headliner was Jackie Mason, a young comedian, who was terrific. While waiting for our car in the parking lot, who approaches me — Jackie Mason. He asked me if I could give him a lift to Long Beach, about ten minutes away. I told him of course we would but only if he put on a show for us in the car. He was funnier in the car than he was on stage!

A few of my friends and me were invited to a party in the Five Towns community of Long Island. It was a nice party, with plenty of snooty people there. With a couple of drinks under his belt, George was feeling aggressive. A couple of hotshot Long Island guys started to give George a bit of a hard time, putting down Brooklyn. George shut these wise guys up by saying, "I can bury you in five dollar bills!"

That was the end of the confrontation!

***

On a snowy Saturday night in early 1963, my friend Brooks' parents were away, so we had a party at his house. George had a little too much to drink (actually, he was loaded), and when the party was over, George slipped on the ice and ripped his pants. His girlfriend Marilyn said that her father could repair the pants so he took them off and gave them to her. I drove her home to Coney Island, along with George. Being in Coney Island on a Saturday night meant going to Nathan's for a hot dog as a nightcap. So there we were at 2 a.m. on a frigid February night eating hot dogs, with George only in his high black socks and overcoat. He was a sight!

***

Kathy and I got married early in 1965 and George, the copycat, married Florence later that year. The next summer, the newlywed Karps rented a beach house in Westhampton with some friends. One Saturday night, we had a big party and George and Florence were invited. One of our fellow renters, Barry had a huge Great Dane, named Dante. As usual, George had a bit too much to drink and was feeling pretty good. The highlight of the party, or even the highlight of the season, was the sight of my friend George dancing with Dante, a huge dog. The fact that Dante was about twelve inches taller than George made a hilarious picture!

***

Around 2005, I became concerned because in speaking to George, I felt that he was not quite understanding what I was saying. Evelyn, his new wife, confided to me that he had been diagnosed with early Alzheimer's disease. Very slowly, he became worse and we all knew what was ahead.

Evelyn and George visited us in Florida where we had dinner one Saturday night. George said to me, "How's your cousin Bob?"

I told him that Bob had passed away ten years earlier. George started to cry, real tears. A few minutes later, he asked me the same question, and I gave him the same answer and George cried again. When he again asked me the same question a few minutes later, I changed my answer and said, "Bob is fine and living in Miami Beach."

George smiled and was so happy.

His condition deteriorated and eventually became terrible. When he passed away, his wife asked if I would deliver the eulogy. Of course I agreed and delivered an upbeat eulogy, consisting of some of the above stories.

I'm sure George understood my humor and was now in heaven, laughing!

HOLD THE MAYO!

A T LINCOLN HIGH School, my modern history class was having its midterm exam. Even then, as a junior, and as I do now, I really liked the subject of history. One historic incident really stands out to me.

One of the questions on the test was on a long, confusing paragraph that was written by Mao Tse Tung, the leader of communist China. The question read, "In this statement, what does Mao mean?"

Our teacher, Mr. Axelrod, read aloud some of the responses to the question. He could not control himself from laughing when he read one of the answers — "Mayonnaise!"

I think the student got extra credit for that answer. After all, his name was Hellman!

A SPECIAL FRIEND

HARVEY WAS A special friend and we had very much in common. As a starter, Harvey's uncle Lou was my father's very best friend when they were young. Pledging our high school fraternity at the same time, Harvey and I endured Hell Night together. Both of us got "paddled" by our new fraternity brothers, at the same time. My tush was sore and purple for a week!

One Saturday, before I got my driver's license, I borrowed my father's big green 1949 Buick to practice my driving. Harvey went with me because he already had a license. I really didn't know how to drive, and I didn't know who was more nervous, Harvey or me. Driving along, I hit a pothole in the street and the car shook. My hubcap went rolling down the street and I said to my friend, "Do I need it?"

"Of course you need it, you idiot. Your father will shoot you if you come home without a hubcap."

I chased the hubcap down the street, caught it, and reattached it.

***

My girlfriend Judy had a friend Lynn and I introduced Harvey to Lynn, and guess what — they became a couple. Lynn felt that my friends and I were a bad influence on Harvey, which was silly, because Harvey was a bad influence on us! They got married soon thereafter, Harvey being the first of the Brighton Boys to get married.

I was an usher at the wedding, along with Brooks and George. The three of us bought new bowties to wear with our rented tuxedos. The newest style from Hollywood was a big oversized bowtie to be worn with a tuxedo. Lynn told me that with the bowtie, I looked like Bozo the Clown!

Harvey and I liked to play practical jokes on each other — mostly me, playing a joke on him.

In 1982, I read in the newspaper that Neil Sedaka had just published an autobiography. I went up to the Macy's bookstore, found the book, and bought it. As I quoted earlier, Neil had written some very nice things about me, and I was very proud of it.

The next day, over lunch with Harvey, I mentioned that Neil had written an autobiography. Harvey and Neil both lived in the same apartment building growing up, and they knew each other pretty well. I suggested to Harvey that we go to Macy's, find the book because maybe Neil had written something about us. We found the book, and Harvey went through it but found only stuff about me and nothing about him. He was upset with me, but I told him it's not my fault, "Neil just thought that I was more interesting than you. Be mad at him, not at me!"

***

Years later, I told Harvey that I had met a terrific lady — Rita. The only downside was that Rita had an eight-year-old daughter. Wisely, Harvey said, " Look at the bright side. In two years, she'll be ten!"

That made a lot of sense.

Businesswise, when I relocated to Florida, I became a financial adviser at A.G. Edwards, and Harvey, as a good friend, became a client. In the late 1990s, Harvey got sick and became sicker. I really made him happy when I came to New York, and arranged a special tour of the New York Stock Exchange. Harvey died in 2002, a sad day for all who knew and loved him. At his funeral, I delivered one of the eulogies.

I miss my special friend!

A great picture of friendship and happiness!
Harvey, George R., and I — 1997 in East Hampton.

BRIGHTON BEACH MEMORIES

THE OCEANA THEATER was the only movie house in Brighton Beach. Right next to the theater was a small luncheonette, Norm & Phil's. When I was a junior in high school, I worked there after school — this was my first executive job.

Norm was really Norma, a big blustery woman who was married to Phil, a skinny cigarette- smoking man, who worked about eighteen hours each day. Their son Marty was a handsome college student with a great personality, who liked to schmooze with the customers. The three of them would argue every day about who was the most important person in the operation. Norma was the cook, and she said her great cooking was the most important thing. Phil said his hard work was the most important, while Marty said his personality and charm were instrumental to the success of the business.

My friend Harvey worked there for about a year for wages that were ridiculously low. To say that the owners were cheap would be an understatement. One lunch hour, the luncheonette was packed and Harvey was scurrying about. He was carrying a hamburger and he accidentally dropped it. Phil was walking by and he stepped on the burger. Now, there was an imprint of a Cat's Paw, from Phil's shoe on the hamburger. Harvey asked Phil what should he do. Phil whispered, "Serve it," and Harvey complied! Harvey said that the customer loved the hamburger and left him a big tip.

When Harvey tired of being underpaid and overworked, he got a new job as CEO of another neighborhood eating spot. He recommended me to replace him and after an extensive interview with the trio, I was hired. My contract called for a starting salary of eleven dollars for a twenty-two hour week, or fifty cents per hour. I worked hard, didn't drop any hamburgers, and the family liked me. At night before closing, Phil would say to me, "Give 'em a sweep."

I grabbed the broom and swept the restaurant clean. After a few months, I worked up the nerve to ask for a raise. Phil told me that I was a good boy and he would give me a two dollar raise. He added that, of course, I would have to work four more hours. I was really happy until I realized that I was still making the same half a buck an hour!

One afternoon, I was in the dressing room changing into my white uniform. The kitchen was in the basement and Norma was cooking up a storm. She started to walk up the stairs, carrying a big roast beef in a pan, when she saw me standing in my underwear. She screamed and dropped the roast beef on to the basement floor. Needless to say, she picked it up and served it, and the customers all loved their roast beef dinner!

When I resigned my position a few weeks later, The Wall Street Journal reported the story.

With me gone, I was very surprised that the luncheonette did not go out of business.

THE DODGERS FINALLY WIN!

"THESE WERE THE best of times, these were the worst of times." I'm not writing about "A Tale of Two Cities," but rather a tale of Brooklyn Dodgers' baseball.

I was a Dodger fan from the time I was born until my favorite team broke my heart and left Brooklyn in 1957 for sunny California, and became the Los Angeles Dodgers. My father was a diehard Dodger fan and I certainly learned from him. I lived and breathed Brooklyn Dodger baseball. Undoubtedly, the Dodgers were the best team in the National League between 1940 and 1956. In that fourteen year period, excluding three war years, the Dodgers finished in third place once, in second place six times, and won the pennant seven times! Unfortunately, in each of the seven World Series that were played, my Dodgers had to play their arch rivals, the New York Yankees. In six of those seven World Series meetings, the Yankees prevailed.

But then, there was 1955. That was the year of the Boys of Summer! The Dodgers won the pennant by a whopping thirteen games. Roy Campanella was the league's "Most Valuable Player"; Duke Snider hit forty-two home runs with 136 RBIs; Carl Furillo batted .314; Gil Hodges had 102 RBIs; and Don Newcombe won twenty games. This had to be the year that the Dodgers would finally beat the Yankees and win their first World Series. The Yankees won the first two games but the Dodgers came back and won the next three games. The Yankees won game six and it all came down to a crucial game seven.

Game seven was played on October 4, my mother's birthday. She told me that morning, "Today is the day of destiny for your team. It's my birthday and I know the Dodgers will win."

My mom knew nothing about baseball, but she was absolutely right. The Boys of Summer celebrated her birthday, and the Dodgers beat the Yankees 2-0! I was outside at the corner candy store with my friends listening to the game on my red Sentinel portable radio. Celebrating, I heaved my radio high into the air and like the great centerfielder Duke Snider, I made a remarkable catch!

Every year that the Dodgers had lost to the Yankees in the World Series, *The Daily News* printed on it's cover, "Wait Till Next Year." Next year had finally arrived!

INSIDE THE GREEN BOX

UNCLE HERMAN WAS married seventy years to Aunt Roselle, my mother's older sister. The sisters were very close and we all lived in the same Brooklyn neighborhood. When they were young, Roselle was ironing clothes one day when my mother approached her and said, "I dare you to iron my hand with the hot iron."

Unfortunately for my mom, Roselle took the dare and for the next sixty years, this story was retold in a heated fashion.

Uncle Herman had a brother-in-law named Irving. Irving was a ne'er-do-well who had some trouble with the law. Whether it was murder, tax evasion, or jaywalking, I am not sure. Irving was a guest of the federal government in prison for a short time. This was a hush-hush matter and my family had no knowledge of this. My father, always the joker, approached Irving at a family gathering and innocently said, "Hi Irving, when did you get out?"

The party ended abruptly!

At Uncle Herman's ninetieth birthday party, his son Burt said, "I would like everyone to tell a humorous story about my father."

This was difficult for some people because Uncle Herman was not a particularly funny person. I racked my brain for a funny incident and told this story:

I was a high school senior and came home from school every day about 4 p.m., usually very hungry. My favorite food with my three glasses of milk was a blackout cake from Ebinger's bakery, which my mother would bring home about once a week. Without a doubt,

Ebinger's was the best bakery in Brooklyn. I could not wait to see the light green Ebinger's box waiting for me when I returned home from school.

That morning, Aunt Roselle told my mother over the phone that Uncle Herman was having a minor operation to remove his hemorrhoids. Mom scribbled the word "HEMORRHOIDS" on the top of the light green Ebinger's box that was next to the telephone. I came home from school, starving, and spotted the light green box. To my dismay, I thought this was a box of hemorrhoids and I refused to open it, fearful of what was inside!

I told this story at the party and got a great laugh. Even old Uncle Herman laughed!

***

I remember telling him that since he was born in 1899, if he lived to the year 2000, he would have lived in three centuries. Obviously, very few people have done that. My Uncle Herman lived to age 100. His birthday was in July; he reached his goal of age 100 and then died in August, just five months shy of the three century mark!

MY HAPPIEST YEAR

L OOKING BACK AT my long life and trying to pinpoint my happiest year, I would say that my senior year in high school was the best. I was sixteen, turning seventeen in February, and I was happy. My grades were good, I knew that I would get into a tuition-free city school, I had lots of friends, and my social life was terrific. The country was not at war, and the Brooklyn Dodgers were world champions. I had no money, and my family's finances were not great, but I didn't care. We had our health, and most importantly, my family was the least dysfunctional family that I would ever see!

I had pledged and was accepted into Lincoln's best fraternity, Sigma Lambda Rho, and I was soon elected Social Director. Whenever I wore my purple and white fraternity sweater, which was daily, I felt that I was the biggest man in school. Dating the best looking girls, who were usually cheerleaders at my school or Madison or Midwood or Lafayette, was very easy for me. I collected many phone numbers of these pretty girls I had met at parties. When the time came to call one for a Saturday night date, if her line was busy, well, I just ripped up her phone number, never to call her again. Sorry to say, I was shallow!

There was a very popular daily television dance program, *The Ted Steele Show*, on channel 11 in New York. One of my fraternity brothers had a connection there, and fifteen members of my fraternity were invited to appear on the program. I invited Gail, a very good dancer, to go with me to the show. I was a good Lindy dancer, but not a great one. Two friends of mine, Harvey and Hank M. were great dancers, and they knew it!

At the end of the program, there was a dance contest and everyone was eager to win the prize. "Rock around the Clock" was playing and everyone was doing their best to win the contest, especially Harvey and Hank. The music stopped, the judge walked around the floor, and who did she pick as the winner — yours truly! My two friends were shocked at the result, and in fact, my friend Harvey did not talk to me for a month!

The prize was a dinner at a French restaurant which we loved. My parents and sister were so proud of me, and the next day in school, I was treated like a celebrity. That was certainly a happy time in my happiest year!

***

Now let's fast-forward twenty-three years to 1978. Harvey, still my very good friend, was turning forty and a surprise party was planned for him. I had a great idea that I knew would make him laugh. I called Western Union a few days before the party, telling them to deliver a telegram to Harvey at exactly 10 p.m. They delivered the telegram and Harvey read aloud, "Sorry for the delay of twenty-three years, but going back over our records and past television programs, it appears that you and **not George Karp**, are the winner of the dance contest."

With that, I presented Harvey with a gold trophy that I had inscribed. He loved it!

But, I was not finished. I called Western Union again and had them deliver a telegram to Harvey a few days later. The telegram read, "We apologize but after rechecking the videotapes, it appears that the winner of the dance contest is *really* George Karp. Please return the trophy."

Harvey laughed for a week!

The best high school fraternity — ever!
Sigma Lambda Rho, 1956.
I am in the front row, second from right, wearing argyle socks.

GO JUMP IN THE LAKE

IT WAS A cold, gray, snowy Sunday afternoon in February of my senior year in high school. Five of my friends and I were deciding what to do on this dismal afternoon. Homework was out of the question, so we decided to take a walk and figure out what to do.

We approached Sheepshead Bay and one of my friends had an idea. Hank U. was a very serious guy and probably the last person to do something "out of this world." In later years, Hank became an attorney and actually successfully handled a law case for my daughter Heather. Looking into the dark and murky water, Hank said, "If everyone gives me a dollar, I'll jump into the Bay."

A dollar was absolutely a lot of money in 1956, but I couldn't resist the idea of seeing someone jumping into the Bay in the middle of February. Hank collected five dollars, took off his jacket and shoes, climbed over the rail, and jumped into the icy, dirty Bay! He climbed out, drenched, and ran home, five dollars richer from his surreal experience. I can not imagine the story that he told his parents.

The next Sunday, with everyone at school having heard about the Bay jumping, about ten of us walked again to Sheepshead Bay. Another friend, Hank M., a very daring and outgoing person said that he would jump in, also for a dollar a man. Money was collected, and Hank jumped in. This was getting to be really interesting!

Sunday next, it was really cold. Not to be outdone, my friend Mel, said that he would take the plunge for money. He stood at the edge and jumped, and just before he hit the water, Hank M. shouted, "We're only kidding, no money for you!"

Mel was not a good swimmer and he was floundering in the icy water. A man and his young son, docked in their rowboat, were watching this ridiculous scene. Mel reached for his boat to pull himself up, and the little boy started to cry because he was frightened. The boy's father picked up an oar and started to hit Mel over the head!

Finally, Mel was able to climb out of the water but with bumps on his head. I figured that he had worked hard, so I gave him the dollar.

My friends asked me if I would jump in the next Sunday.

"Sorry," I lied, "I have to do my homework!"

THE MATH CLASS

O NE OF THE highlights of my senior year in high school was my math class. This was an honors class for the best math students in our grade. The class was taught by Miss Goldberg, who was the best looking young teacher in Lincoln. My friend Rick, who is now a Boca Raton neighbor of mine, always teased me and told me that Miss Goldberg really liked me and why don't I ask her out for a date. I was seventeen and she was probably twenty-five, so I didn't think that was a great idea.

For some reason, I became the class comedian, and I must say that I was pretty funny. One day, Miss Goldberg was working me over for not handing in an assignment. In her squeaky voice, she said, "George, I am going to call your mother."

With the whole class listening, I responded, " Good…Could you please tell her to get my new pants out of the cleaners!"

The class broke up and even Miss Goldberg could not help laughing.

***

Every year on a Saturday night before graduation, the school put on a production called "Senior Class Night." The producers of the show knew about our famous math class, and they decided to do a skit about the class. My friend and classmate Neil Sedaka did the music and it was terrific. Although I wasn't in the show as an actor, I was a featured performer. Peter, who portrayed me in the skit, borrowed my fraternity sweater to wear onstage. The whole school attended the show and it was a great success. Of course, I loved the skit about the math class. It propelled me into a "minor" celebrity!

Go forward about six years, and I was standing in the lobby of the Concord Hotel when I heard a squeaky voice that I immediately recognized. It was the famous Miss Goldberg! We both were very happy to see each other after so many years, and I think that she was very proud of me, knowing that I had just graduated from college.

Now go forward another fifty years. After tennis one day, my friend Frank and I were discussing growing up in New York. When he learned that I went to Lincoln, he asked me if I knew his cousin, Miss Millie Goldberg. I told him of course I did, and I related some of the funny stories of the math class.

He told me that she had died a few years ago, and truth be told, I felt really sad!

YOUNG SANDY KOUFAX

DURING THE WINTER of my senior year in high school, I attended a basketball game between my school, Lincoln, and our archrival, Lafayette. Our gym was packed and who was sitting in front of me? — none other then the former Lafayette basketball player, who was now pitching for the world champion Brooklyn Dodgers — Sandy Koufax.

I was thinking of a way to get his attention and in a loud voice, I said to my friend sitting next to me, "The baseball season starts very soon. If only the Dodgers had a good left-handed pitcher, they might win the World Series again."

I got his attention all right, and the future Hall of Famer gave me a dirty look. I think he would have liked to bean me with a ninety-five mile-per-hour fastball!

I WAS A TEENAGE BULLY

I DO NOT KNOW if there is a statute of limitations on bullying, but I hope there is. After sixty years, I admit that I bullied someone, and I'm terribly sorry that I did.

Bob Z. was a "nebbish" — we knew it and he knew it. He was short, he was fat, he had terrible eyesight, and he wore thick glasses. Besides that, his personality was minimal. He was not exactly the most popular kid in school.

Bob wanted very much to be accepted by my friends and me. We knew and he knew that he would be the scapegoat for all of our pranks, and he readily accepted this. We worked him over, incessantly, and he always came back for more.

BOB, I'M SORRY! If you happen to read this book, I hope you can accept my sincere apology, after so many years.

ELVIS THE PELVIS

ELVIS PRESLEY RUINED my love life!

I met Dorothy, a great-looking cheerleader from Madison High School, when I was sixteen, at a party in January 1956. I made a date with her for the next Saturday night, and I was really looking forward to it. On this particular Saturday night, Elvis Presley was appearing on television for the first time, on the *Dorsey Brothers show* at 8 p.m. Elvis was just starting to get very popular and "Heartbreak Hotel" was quickly moving up the charts. I told Dorothy that I would pick her up at 8 o'clock and I did not want to be late. But, I just had to see Elvis! My friend Mel, who lived in the same building as me, insisted that I watch Elvis with him. We watched the first few minutes and then I raced from his house to the bus stop.

I got to Dorothy's house at 9 o'clock, only one hour late, and I rang the bell. Her mother castigated me and told me her daughter was sleeping. Dorothy came down the steps in her flannel pajamas and told me never to call her again. Yes, Elvis had ruined my love life!

I told my kids this story many times. I told them that Elvis the Pelvis had a brother named Enos. They always laughed!

***

Now, let's go back to the future only sixty years! My three wonderful daughters came to Florida to celebrate their favorite father's 75th birthday! I picked up Heather at the airport, and Jennifer and Vanessa cryptically told me that when I came back from the airport, I should ring the bell and not walk right in.

I rang the bell and Elvis Presley answered. Well, he looked like Elvis and he dressed like Elvis and he sang like Elvis, but since I knew that he was dead thirty-seven years, I figured he was not Elvis!

The party was fun, with lots of my friends in attendance, listening to the pseudo-Elvis sing "Hound Dog," "Don't be Cruel," "Heartbreak Hotel," and about fifty other songs.

Elvis and my daughters made this a very special day!

George and Elvis singing together in 2014.
Elvis was standing on my Blue Suede Shoes!

STOMACH TROUBLE

M Y FRIEND JACK lived on the next block (Brighton 11th Street) and he was always trying to pull a fast one on me. Finally, I got my revenge or at least I thought I did.

We were seniors in high school and graduation was only a week away. Jack was absent one day, and the next day when he returned, we were all sitting in the lunchroom. When he walked away from the table, I noticed a letter sticking out of his book. His mother had written an excuse note to his teacher saying that Jack had an upset stomach and couldn't come to school that day.

I took the note and on the bottom I wrote, *"He didn't shit for a week."*

I put the note back in Jack's book and figured that he would have a good laugh out of it. The next day, while I was in class, a messenger came in and told my teacher that the Boy's Dean wanted to see me. Now, I was nervous and fearful that Jack had gotten me into trouble. The dean really let me have it, telling me my conduct was disgraceful and I was not going to graduate.

Shaking, I left the room not knowing what to do. Now I was the one having stomach trouble!

Finally, the dean came out, put his arm around me, and told me it was all a joke.

Jack had gotten me again!

THE IDEA MAN

I WAS ALWAYS PRETTY good with coming up with an idea; in fact, Rita's daughter Stephanie called me "The Idea Man!"

Just before high school graduation in the spring of 1956, I had an idea and it ultimately worked. I needed a job for the summer, but I knew it would be tough getting one. Since it would only be for two months as I would be starting college that September, I didn't think that companies would be happy with my long term goals. My idea was to go to a skyscraper building in Manhattan, start at the top floor and knock on every door in the building, attempting to get a job.

I went to the Woolworth Building in lower Manhattan, did a lot of knocking and interviewing, and happily got a job with the Union Bag and Paper Company. The personnel manager was impressed with me and asked me if I would be going to college. I told him a small lie and said that I would be taking night classes. He offered me an executive job, in the mailroom, and I happily accepted.

I had to pick up and deliver mail from every office every hour. Too bad emails were not invented in 1956! An older woman, about forty, who I thought might be a Nazi spy, looked at me suspiciously every day. She asked me questions about my name, my parents, and where were they born. When I told the anti-Semitic bitch, "My mother was born in South Dakota and my father was born in West Virginia," she then asked me where were my grandparents from.

This was starting to resemble the Spanish Inquisition. I looked the inquisitor right in the eye and said, "One set of grandparents were from New Zealand and the other set of grandparents were from Greenland."

This satisfied her anti-Semitic curiosity and she never bothered me again!

Going to work on the subway one morning, I was talking to a classmate of mine, Eric. I told him that I was really busy in the mailroom sorting out proxies, whatever they were. Eric's father worked on Wall Street and Eric knew exactly what a proxy was. I was very naïve and did not know that my company was being bought out. I assume Eric and his father made a tidy profit on my inside information to him. I never did visit Eric in prison!

City College of New York (CCNY), the college of my choice, was starting classes in mid-September. I gathered my strength and went to the personnel manager, who had hired me a few months before. I explained that I had decided not to go to night school but instead I would go to day school. Therefore, I would be resigning my executive position at the mailroom in two weeks. He was very disappointed with my decision, and as soon as the news hit *The Wall Street Journal*, the company's stock fell twenty points!

The Jewish holiday Rosh Hashanah was celebrated the next week, and I took off two days from work to join in the celebration. On my final day of work, I received my last paycheck and unbelievably saw that I was not paid for the two days that I was gone from work. To say the least, I was pissed!

The Idea Man had an idea and revenge was on my mind.

On my last round of picking up the mail, back at the mailroom, I purposely put every letter into the wrong letterbox. On the next Monday morning, Union Bag and Paper Company would be in a turmoil. The old "waspy" Manhattan company would remember the nice Jewish boy from Brooklyn!

Revenge was sweet!

FROM LEMONS TO LEMONADE

O NE OF MY good friends through my high school and college
years was Sheldon. He lived on the next block from me, and
we had a lot of good times and laughs together.

The summer after I graduated high school was a great one for me.
I was working in downtown Manhattan, as was my friend Sheldon.
One day, we met for lunch at the Automat, but we brought our own
sandwiches. I noticed that there were glasses with ice cubes, to be used
for iced tea, on the counter. Next to the glasses was a large bowl of
lemons, again for the iced tea.

Sheldon thought it would be a great idea if we took the lemons and
ice cubes and made lemonade. We were casually guzzling lemonade,
but the manager did not like the idea and politely threw us out. Had
anyone ever been kicked out of the Automat? I doubt it!

Sheldon, unlike me, was not a baseball fan. But, he was a joker. He
surprised me in October 1956 when he told me that he was happy that
the World Series was starting tomorrow because he loved the Yankees.
Besides Mickey Mantle and Yogi Berra, I was sure that he could not
name any of the other twenty-three players on the Yankees roster.
He told me that he could name the whole team which I thought was
preposterous. We made a bet (a dime a name), and he proceeded to
name all of the Yankees causing me to lose two dollars and thirty cents.
He had memorized the roster and suckered me into the bet. Whenever
I see him, I tell him that he owes me two dollars and thirty cents +
interest!

We started CCNY together and the highlight of my brief time there was that on Thursdays, there were no classes in the afternoon. Sheldon and I would walk through Harlem to 125th Street, buy balcony seats at the Apollo theater, eat our sandwiches and see great Rock 'n Roll shows. We saw Fats Domino, the Platters, Frankie Lymon, etc. That was the best!

We were coming home from school one day on the subway, and I was taking my daily nap, instead of studying. While I was sleeping, Sheldon had a demented idea, and on all the advertisements in the subway car he scribbled, " FOR A GOOD TIME, CALL ARLENE AT NI 8-2762."

My sister Arlene was nine years old at the time!

I think Harvey saw the sign, called her and they eventually got married and lived happily ever after!

GRANNY & THE DODGERS

T HEY SAY THINGS happen in three. I think they're right!

1) I had just started college in September 1956 when one morning my mother got a phone call that her mother, Granny, had passed away in her sleep. I was very close to my grandmother and I took the news very hard.

The funeral was to be the next day, and I was chosen to be the bearer of bad news to my grandmother's friends. My mother gave me a handful of dimes and the phone numbers of some of Granny's cronies that I had to call. I made all the calls, and to say the least, I was very uncomfortable in doing so.

2) I didn't go to school that day and I was really "down in the dumps." That afternoon I went downstairs to get the mail and there was a letter addressed to me. I opened it and it blew my mind!

I had won a New York State Regents scholarship for $1,400. I was rich!

My parents were ecstatic — so very proud of me. Mom told me, " Granny's looking out for you. She is in heaven and she made this happen."

I ran down Brighton 12th Street and went to all my friends apartments, Hank, Shelly, Natie, and Mel, to tell them about my good news. I think they were all happy for me. They were real friends.

3) The third thing happened that night. My Brooklyn Dodgers were in a tight fight to win the pennant. This was the end of the season and every game was so important to the team and to me. In honor

of my grandmother, who didn't know a baseball from a matzoh ball, the Dodgers beat the Phillies that night. But the way they did it was unbelievable. Sal Maglie, the Dodger pitcher, pitched a no-hitter — for my grandmother!

Granny made it happen!

NO BUSINESS LIKE SNOW BUSINESS

OORAY, FINAL EXAMS are over!

I had just completed my first semester in college. I sweated through finals in math, chemistry, philosophy, etc., and now I had to wait for my grades to come by way of a postcard. I collected the mailbox keys from my parents so I could see the postcards first. However, the mailman and the yentas in my apartment building, who hung around the lobby mailbox, would be the first to see my grades. I dreaded the idea of Mrs. Schwartz calling my mother to say that George got a "D" in sex hygiene!

It was mid-January and the snow was falling. I was out with my friends to celebrate the end of finals, and we came up with a plan to make some money. We decided to shovel snow the next morning in Manhattan Beach. I lived in Brighton Beach and because there were so many apartment houses, there was no opportunity to shovel snow there. Manhattan Beach was made up of private homes and was the most affluent neighborhood in Brooklyn. Residents there were definitely not snow shovelers!

A few of my friends, (Mel, Harvey, Hank M.) and I met at 9 a.m. to do some serious shoveling, something that none of us had ever done before. I realized that in order to do shoveling, one had to have a shovel. My younger sister Arlene had a shovel but it was a trifle small since she used it to play at the seashore during the summer.

I racked my seventeen-year-old brain and came up with a great idea. There had to be a big shovel in the basement of my apartment house that the superintendent Henry, would use for his chores. I figured that he had plenty of shovels and he wouldn't mind me borrowing one, so in fact I did borrow one. My friends and I trudged through the snow, shovels held over our shoulders like army rifles and walked the short distance to the opportunities of Manhattan Beach.

I rang the first doorbell to ask if they wanted their driveway shoveled. The lady said, "I don't want to talk to you, I only want to talk to your boss."

The "boss" was my friend Mel, who was wearing his father's hat, which made him look older. So, he became the boss and he negotiated all of our transactions that day. I never worked so hard for so little money, but between snowball fights and rolling in the snow, I had a great time!

Hunger, frostbite, and fatigue overtook us, and we decided to call it a day at 2 o'clock. We figured that we would splurge and have a great meal at Kwai Fong, the best Chinese restaurant in Brighton. I threw my borrowed shovel under a snow covered car near the restaurant figuring that I would pick it up later. We did have a great meal.

Unaccustomed to working so hard and to eating so much, I became very tired and a nap at home was necessary. I was in the deepest sleep when my father awakened me by shouting, "What the hell have you done? There is no heat in the building and the neighbors are rioting in the lobby. **And, they're blaming you!**"

It seems that one of the neighbors saw me with the shovel in the morning and now I was being judged guilty, without a trial. I found out that my shovel was the only shovel in the basement, and Henry the superintendent, would not load coal into the furnace by hand. My father made me go down to the street and retrieve our only shovel, except I was not sure just where it was. After an hour, searching under snow covered cars, I found the elusive shovel and brought it back to the building, where several of my frostbitten neighbors greeted me, unkindly.

Analyzing that experience, I think that is the reason I now live in Florida!

LULLABY OF BIRDLAND

A s one gets older, one changes in many ways. My taste in music was now evolving from Rock 'n Roll, and now at age eighteen, I started to really like jazz. I would go to jazz concerts, jazz clubs, and listen to late-night jazz on the radio. Miles Davis, the Modern Jazz Quartet, and Dizzy Gillespie were my new heroes.

One Saturday night, my friends and I went to Birdland, a famous jazz club in Manhattan. Count Basie was playing and Joe Williams was his singer, and the club was packed. A person could sit at a table, order a meal, and have expensive drinks. Or, a practical person could stand at the bar, the Bullpen, and sip a Pepsi.

I was that practical person.

Standing next to me at the bar, was an older black man, who was pretty drunk. When Joe Williams sang a fast song, the man, wearing hightop basketball sneakers, jumped up and down. When Joe Williams sang a slow, sad ballad, the old man started to cry. I remember tears running down his face.

Now let's go forward about thirty years. While waiting for a flight at the Las Vegas airport, I noticed an older Joe Williams reading a newspaper. I approached the famous singer, told him that I recognized him, and said that I was a fan of his for many years. He was very cordial and we had a nice conversation.

I told him about that night at Birdland and the old man who was laughing and then crying. The famous singer loved the story!

Joe Williams died about ten years later. Every time they play a Joe

Williams song on satellite radio, I still remember the old man laughing and crying.

STANDING ON THE CORNER

M Y FRIENDS AND I wanted to continue the good times that we had experienced in high school. So even though we all went to different colleges, in 1957 we formed our own college fraternity called the "Distinguished Men's Social Club" or Delta Mu Sigma Chi. I was elected Social Director and I arranged parties with sororities from many different high schools every Friday night. Sometimes, I arranged two parties the same night, home and away. We rented a basement on a residential street, Dahill Road, that became our club house.

One Friday evening, while everyone was slow dancing, with raging hormones, to the Platters or Johnny Mathis, suddenly one of the basement windows was kicked in from the outside.

A group of gentlemen, not exactly from Harvard or Yale, wearing black motorcycle jackets, entered our party uninvited. "Hey man, we don't want youze guys taking over our corner," their leader, clearly not an English major, said.

One of our boys bravely replied, "Gentlemen, we are not interested in taking over your corner. We're in the middle of the block, and we never go to the corner. We just want to have a good time with our girlfriends. Would you like to have a beer or a Pepsi?"

These wiseguys stayed at the party and had a great time and we all became friends. In fact, they all wanted to join our fraternity, but we told them sorry — motorcycles were not allowed!

TAPESTRY

THE YEAR WAS 1957. A skinny fifteen-year-old girl from James Madison High School liked my friend Sid. The girl could play the piano very well and really knew how to sing, especially songs that she had written.

She was friendly with my friend Neil Sedaka, who was yet to become a star. The skinny girl invited Sid to her house one afternoon, and as a good friend, Sid the Kid, asked her to bring a friend for me. The friend was chubby, unattractive, and could not play the piano nor sing. We did not hit it off, and I couldn't wait to get out of there.

By the way, the name of the skinny girl who liked Sid was Carol Klein.

She later changed her name to Carol King!

DECEMBER SUNSTROKE

M Y FIRST YEAR at college was spent at CCNY Uptown, which was on 138th Street in Manhattan. By the end of the first week of school, I hated it and had to move on, or so I thought. Living in Brighton Beach and traveling by subway to school was an unbelievable event, taking almost an hour and a half each way. Walking through the neighborhood around the school was scary, and it seemed to rain every day.

Now for the bad parts. At Lincoln high school, I was a social person and I knew all the younger girls. At CCNY, I was a just a kid and all the freshmen girls were interested in juniors and seniors. I was not a happy camper! I wanted to transfer to Brooklyn College immediately, but I was told that I could not transfer until the following September. I endured my freshman year at CCNY, and the following September I enrolled at Brooklyn College, only fifteen minutes from my house. I liked the school, made many friends, and met plenty of girls.

The end of the first semester at Brooklyn College arrived, and I had many tests that I had to prepare for. At this time, my father hurt his back and a friend of his gave him a heat lamp for treatment. The back of the heat lamp was a sun lamp that I was anxious to use, to get a tan on my pale face, during the winter season. I sat under the lamp for a few minutes, following the instructions which said to use carefully for only five minutes. After five minutes, I looked in the mirror and saw that I was paler than before. Figuring that it was not working, I lay down on the couch watching TV, under the sun lamp for about an hour.

The next morning my face was a little pink but by evening my face got red, and I started to shake and shiver. I went to bed covered with about five blankets and I was still freezing. The next morning, my mother called the doctor who quickly made a house call (in those days doctors came to a patient's house). In jest I said, "Doc, I think I have a sunstroke."

He said, "You're absolutely right. You're the first person ever to have a sunstroke in New York in December!"

***

Final exams were almost here, and my eyes were so swollen that I could not see. I asked my mother if she could read to me, and of course she agreed. For my English class, I had to study "Hamlet," so Mom began to read Shakespeare to me. Hamlet says to Ophelia, "Get thee to a nunnery."

I asked Mom innocently, "What is a nunnery?"

Mom looked it up in the dictionary (no Google yet), and her face turned redder than my face. In a very embarrassed voice, she said, "It means whorehouse."

After taking a deep breath she asked, "Now can we study geography?"

YOU CAN TAKE THE BOY OUT OF BROOKLYN

Talk about being naïve and sheltered!

Living in Brooklyn as a youth, I had little to do with the borough of Manhattan. In my juvenile mind, I knew that people worked in Manhattan in large office buildings. I thought that people who lived in Manhattan were poor and lived only on the lower East side. I soon realized that there was another side to Manhattan.

When I was about eighteen, I met a girl Toni at a fraternity party. I liked her and asked her out on a date for the following week. She lived in Manhattan but not on the lower East side, but rather the upper East side. I found my way to her apartment building on Park Avenue and conceded that it was nicer than my apartment building on Brighton 12th Street. The man in uniform guarding the building, the doorman, told me that she lived on the 10th floor. When I asked him what was the apartment number, the doorman just repeated, "Tenth floor." There was another uniformed man in the elevator, the elevator operator, who took me to the 10th floor. We certainly did not have an elevator operator in my building; only my neighbor Mr. Goldberg liked to hang out there and ride our dilapidated elevator, up and down, up and down.

The door opened and there I was in Toni's living room. The apartment was huge — everyone in the family had their own bedroom and bathroom. And, the apartment was air-conditioned!

I was totally impressed!

Unfortunately, Toni was not as nice as her apartment, and we never went out again.

I went back to my apartment in Brooklyn, feeling happy, and vowing in the future, to only go out with Brooklyn girls.

LEARNING TO DRIVE

THERE WAS A funny movie called *Learning to Drive* that was released about three years ago. I was one of the very few people that saw it. My own experience of learning to drive in 1958 was pretty memorable.

My friend George R. and I decided to go to a driving school in Brighton, where we could learn the fundamentals of driving. I had driven with my father, and both he and I had gotten a little nervous with my driving. I don't know where I got the money to attend driving school, but it was not very expensive, so I enrolled.

The man who owned the school (not really a school) was named Maurice and he was totally deaf. He would lip read and he was able to speak to us. George and I took lessons together — I would drive and my friend would be in the backseat. He would scream in Maurice's ear, and of course Maurice would not respond. To say the least, George and I did not say the nicest things to Maurice!

I practiced driving with my father in his 1949 big Buick sedan. This huge old car did not have power steering and parking this monster was impossible. Not being the best parallel parker, I finally succeeded, sweating profusely; it was like having spent three hours in the gym!

Practice makes perfect, but as a driver, I practiced, but I was certainly not perfect!

When it was time for my driving test, I borrowed my dad's car that day for the exam, and I recruited my friend Roger to go with me. I was a sophomore at Brooklyn College, having just transferred there, and

Roger was my classmate. I scheduled the test for a weekday afternoon, after school. Since it was a school day, I was not dressed formally, which in retrospect, was a mistake. My dirty white buck shoes did not make much of an impression on the tester.

The person testing me took me to a residential area, and I drove around very nicely. He told me to make a broken U-turn, which I had practiced for weeks. I started to back up slowly, and I went and I went and I went until the tester told me to stop because I was up on somebody's lawn and almost in their living room. Needless to say, I failed!

A few weeks later, I made another appointment to take the test. At my father's insistence, he told me not to go with my friend but to go with him. Dad also told me to wear a jacket and a tie, and of course I agreed. I took the test and drove confidently, and when it was time to make the broken U-turn, I did it flawlessly. When I finished, I saw my father talking to the tester and they became great friends. I was delighted when I learned that I had passed, and now I could finally drive legally.

When I told my friends that I had gotten my license, and now I could be the designated driver, they all said that they would rather take the bus!

THE BORSCHT BELT

I N 1958, THE Passover holiday was a very important event for me. Not because I was religious, which I wasn't, but because it gave me the opportunity to make some much-needed money. Since I was now driving my father's car, the old 1949 Buick that leaked oil, his auto insurance went sky high. My dad told me that if I wanted to drive his car, I had to pay for my share of the car insurance. The best way for me to make one hundred dollars quickly was either to rob a bank or get a job. A nice Jewish boy from Brooklyn does not rob banks!

The year before, for Passover, two of my friends Hank U. and Sheldon, and I worked as busboys at a dinky hotel in the Catskill mountains and made very little money. This year, I decided that I would work in a fancy hotel in the mountains and make some serious money.

Getting a job as a waiter or a busboy in the "Borscht Belt" was as difficult as getting a job in the White House, unless your uncle was named Eisenhower! There was one employment agency in New York City that did all the hiring for the Catskill hotels, the Jupiter Agency. But, in order to get a job, a person needed experience, so telling a few little lies to the interviewer was imperative. A friend of mine had worked the summer before at the Concord Hotel, and he gave me a list to memorize of all the important employees at the Concord.

I made an appointment with the agency and the interviewer barraged me with questions regarding my fake employment last summer at the Concord. I would rather he had asked me questions like, "What is the capital of Mongolia?" and I would have answered, "Ulaanbaatar."

"Who is the head waiter?" he asked.

"Irving Schwartz," I answered.

"Who is the maître d'?"

"Morris Goldberg."

"And who is the head busboy?"

"Melvin Cohen," I replied to his third degree questioning.

So I lied a little; the grand inquisitor was impressed and offered me a job as a busboy at the Pines Hotel, an upscale hotel in the Catskills. While taking the bus from Manhattan to my destination, I met a guy who was going to work at the Pines with me. He was Italian, came from Brooklyn, and went to NYU. His name was SAL and he said to me, "Please do me a favor — when we get to the hotel, please call me SOL."

Sal or Sol knew just how his matzoh was buttered!

I reported for duty the afternoon of the first day of the Passover holiday. Since I was the new kid on the block, I was awarded the worst section of the dining room, which was the farthest from the kitchen. After the Passover services were finished, the plan was that each busboy would march out of the kitchen, carrying a large tray with food and wine bottles on his shoulder. Since my station was the farthest from the kitchen, I had to go first, with the spotlight on me. I never had lifted a tray before and I was sure that a catastrophe was going to happen. But, nervous and sweating, I made it!

The first morning, a guest with a thick European accent said to me, "Sonny boy, can you please bring me an order of PLUNES."

I made him repeat this twice, and I said to him, "We have plums and we have prunes. Which one would you like?"

He responded, "I'll have the PLUNES."

I brought him an order of plums and an order of prunes.

Later he asked me directions for the men's room!

It was a tough week for me as I was working about twelve hours a day. Finally, the last day arrived, which was going to be the big day that everyone would give me a tip for services rendered. Wearing a white jacket with many pockets, my plan was that each guest's tip would go into a different pocket. Shapiro would go top left, Finkelstein bottom right, etc. Right after lunch, I was bombarded with envelopes from each guest, and I put each one into the designated pocket.

In the corner of the dining room, I emptied my pockets and said to myself, Two dollars from Levine, three dollars from Goldstein, etc. Everything was accounted for except for the empty pocket from Kaplan. Not being shy, I went into the main lobby where all the guests were saying their goodbyes. I spotted Mr. and Mrs. Kaplan and asked them if they had enjoyed their vacation at the Pines. They said yes and then I asked if they were happy with my service. They said that I was terrific and then I blurted out, "Then why didn't you tip me?"

"Of course we did," Mr. Kaplan said.

"No, you didn't!"

"Yes, I did".

With that, Mr. Kaplan clutched his chest and went down on one knee. Mrs. Kaplan screamed and I took off. I hid in the big refrigerator room for about an hour, turning purple. When I finally came out, all the guests had gone and the action was over. But I realized, that I had put two tips into one pocket, and so I owed the Kaplans an apology.

The maître d' was furious with me and told me that fortunately Mr. Kaplan was okay. He told me in no uncertain terms that I would never work at the Pines Hotel ever again.

My busboy career was over and I couldn't be happier!

WATERFRONT DIRECTOR

STARTING IN 1958, I was without my beloved baseball team, the Brooklyn Dodgers. The Boys of Summer had deserted me, leaving sunny and warm Brooklyn for damp and cold Los Angeles!

The good news that summer was I had managed to get a great job in the Catskill Mountains. I worked at the Hotel Evans in Loch Sheldrake, New York. My official title was Waterfront Director, and I was in charge of the twenty rowboats on the lake. I was also on the social staff, where my job was to dance and socialize with the young female guests. I had my own room and I ate three big meals a day in the main dining room with the paying guests. This was the ideal job for a nineteen year old, or even for a seventy-eight year old!

My boss, Shelly, hired me after meeting me at Brooklyn College. He told me that I would have a great summer, but I would not be making very much money. After working a week, I realized that he was right, and I would not be making very much money, at all. But, the idea man had a great idea, and it worked!

Down by the lake, guests would take out rowboats for a spin around the lake. When they returned the boat, they thanked me, but never gave me a tip. So from the tobacco shop, I got an empty cigar box that contained the most expensive cigars. The price of each cigar was twenty-five cents and it was marked in big letters on the box. Each morning, I took three or four quarters and put them in the box. People returning their boats started to get the idea and now they would throw their quarters into the box. After two or three weeks, I accumulated some wealth, even though on some days the guests would *take* my quarters!

The hotel had a Latin mambo band, and I became friendly with a few of the musicians. One Monday afternoon, a band member asked me if he could take out a boat. There was no rule that said an employee could not take out a boat, so I agreed and gave him one. When he returned, he gave me a dollar tip and asked if next week he could bring a few friends. Thinking of the dollar tip, I said sure. The next week, he brought five friends with their girlfriends, and I gave them five boats, and when they returned, they gave me five dollars.

Everyone was very happy and the next week, ten musicians showed up. I gave them boats; they were drinking and whatever, and I was well tipped. By the end of the summer, Monday was Musicians Day and Latin musicians from all the hotels in the mountains were coming to go rowing in my lake — Lake George! I was the most popular Waterfront Director in New York State!

My parents and sister came to see me one weekend. But instead of driving the big, green 1949 Buick, my father was driving a 1955 shiny black and white Buick convertible. This was the nicest surprise of the summer, and I couldn't wait to go home to drive the flashy convertible.

The only downside to my job was that when it rained, I had to bail out all the boats with a small pail. When it did rain, the guests would see a movie in the hotel playhouse. Unfortunately, the hotel had only one film and I (ironically) saw *On the Waterfront* about twenty times!

When I returned home to Brighton Beach, being used to a five course dinner, I was disappointed that my meal was only a one course dinner. When I asked my mother if she could serve me fruit soup as an appetizer, she told me to go back to the Hotel Evans!

CHRISTMAS AT MACY'S

I T WAS *THE Miracle on 34th Street.*

I got a job at Macy's, the biggest and best department store in the country.

My dad (1) was friendly with a man (2) whose wife (3) had a cousin (4) who knew a lady (5) who worked at Macy's department store. Knowing that I was anxious to make some money over the Christmas holiday, Dad was instrumental in getting me an interview and ultimately being hired at Macy's. My work schedule was working all day Saturday and a few days during the week, all for the minimum wage — one dollar per hour. But, I really liked the job!

I was lucky in being stationed in a department that I liked. It could have been pots and pans, or ladies undergarments, or garbage disposals, but no — they put me in musical instruments which included the record department. I learned how to work the cash register and I never saw so much money in all my life!

An old Puerto Rican man came in one day, barely able to speak English. He was poorly dressed, and he came in with his young grandson. He explained to me, in very broken English, that he wanted to buy a set of drums for his grandson. Macy's carried several sets of drums and all were very costly. I showed him all the different models, and he chose the most expensive one. Since American Express and other credit cards were not invented in 1958, he paid with cash. From his old wallet, he took out about two hundred dollars, mostly all in singles, and he wanted to do something special for this little boy. I only hope that the boy appreciated his grandfather's generosity, and that this little boy grew into a man who was as good and generous as his grandfather. I was really touched by this!

Working in the record department was fun. The big song that Christmas was "The Chipmunk Song," and it played over and over on the speaker system in the store. "Alvin" was heard every two minutes every day. I, myself, must have sold ten thousand copies!

The store was packed the whole month of December, and I had never seen so many people, pushing and shoving. January came — the crowds left and so did I.

But I remember well the Christmas of 1958 — "Alvin" and the man with the drums!

KEEP THE FAITH

I CHANGED SCHOOLS YET again in my junior year of college (1959), now attending the Baruch School of CCNY. The college was located on East 23rd Street in Manhattan, and the closest it came to being an out-of-town school with a campus, was that it had green linoleum in the lounge! I changed my major from chemistry to business administration, majoring in advertising. I took several advertising courses and really enjoyed them.

I met a pretty girl named Faith, and we both liked each other very much. The best part of this early relationship was the fact that she told me that her father was in the advertising business. I figured that perhaps he could help me in my fledgling advertising career.

I made a date with Faith and picked her up on a Saturday evening, when she introduced me to her father. I told him that I was pleased to meet him and had heard that he was in the advertising business. He responded, "Are you kidding? Advertising? I am in the appetizing business. I sell bagels and lox!"

***

Now fast-forward twenty years and I have nothing to do with advertising. It's a warm, sunny spring day in early June and I am feeling good. I'm wearing a cream-colored suit and have a great suntan, walking down Broadway, near my office. That afternoon my phone rings and after twenty years, Faith is calling to say that her friend saw me that morning and that I was looking good. Briefly, she told me about her life which was really sad. She was a single mom, widowed at a young age. I told her that I was happily married with three kids.

Out of the blue, Faith blurted, "Do you cheat?"

I quickly responded, "Do you mean at tennis?"

She hung up abruptly and I never heard from her again!

Keep the faith, Faith!

BOB COMES FULL CIRCLE

MY COUSIN BOB was a very important person in my life. He was ten years older than me and he actually was a father figure to me. His mother was my mother's sister, and our families were very close, both living in the same Brighton Beach apartment building. Bob's relationship with his father was not good, but his relationship with my parents was excellent.

When I was a junior in college, my mother asked Bob if he could give me a job to keep me off the streets. Bob was running a garment business, and he said "absolutely yes" to her request. I worked after school, learned the business, and I loved it. In December, I was given a very important work assignment. Every year the company hosted a Christmas party for buyers and suppliers. I was put in charge of the Christmas party and had to buy food, provide music, and supply alcoholic refreshments. Most importantly, I had to invite many of my young good-looking female friends, which I did. The party was a great success because of the ladies, and everyone could hardly wait until the next Christmas party!

***

I had graduated college and my active army career was over, when Bob informed me that he was starting a new garment business. He asked me if I would like to join the brand-new company as its first employee. "When do I start?", I replied.

Those early years were the happiest years for me in my business career.

Early in the life of the business, Bob and I went to see a customer one morning on West 34th Street. We passed a Sabretts hotdog stand and Bob was salivating. He ordered one, smothered with onions and sauerkraut, which he devoured. His second one was eaten even more quickly. He could not understand why I was not eating one, and I explained that it was 10 a.m. and I had just eaten my breakfast of Cheerios.

"Philosophically," Bob said, "a person can only be successful in this business only if he eats these hot dogs." I told him that I would take my chances by not eating these delicacies. As a postscript, Bob did not come to work for two days because of a severe upset stomach!

Attempting to do business, we developed a garment that went into the lingerie department of our customers. I went to see the buyer at Lerner shops, a very major customer. The buyer liked our garment, a robe, and called her assistant into the room to model it. The assistant, who was great-looking, came into the room wearing just her underwear. My eyes popped out of my head! I got the order but that was secondary.

I came back to the office, told the story, and Bob said that he and I must go back tomorrow to see this spectacle again. We showed a new garment, and predictably, the assistant came into the room wearing just her underwear, and Bob could not believe it. When we left, he asked me if we could come back again tomorrow!

One day, Bob and I had an appointment to see the buyer at Woolco Stores (of blessed memory). The buyer was an unattractive, obese woman, who had a terrible attitude. When she saw us, unbelievably she said, "Look who's here — Shit and Mud!"

I looked at Bob and asked, "Which one are you?"

***

We had a customer who owned a chain of out-of-town stores. Whenever he came to our office, he said the same hilarious thing.

"How's business?" I would ask.

Predictably, he would answer, "Terrific! Next week will be better."

Bob and I drove to Delaware to visit a factory that we hired to manufacture our product. The factory owner, Mr. Levine, drove us around to show us this quaint Delaware town. I jokingly asked Mr. Levine, "Where is the Jewish Center?"

He responded, "You're looking at him!"

***

One of the pleasures that Bob had was betting on college football games. He thought that he knew all about college football, and it would be easy for him to win, which did not happen very often. Sometimes, he wagered on obscure schools and usually lost. He thought that I knew a lot about the colleges, and one day he asked me what I thought of Colgate. I answered, "They're good, but Pepsodent is better!"

Bob was the best man at my first wedding. I was the best man at his second wedding. His second marriage did not last very long and I introduced him to wife number three. Ultimately, I became a partner in the business and really got to know Bob. He was smart, creative, and successful, and we had lots of laughs at work. After I retired and left the company, bad times overtook him in business, and he became ill and ultimately died.

Bob used to tell me that he had diapered me as an infant, and now here I was delivering the eulogy at his funeral. He had come full circle.

Bob, I miss you!

THE BROTHER I NEVER HAD

M Y SISTER ARLENE is great and I love her dearly, but I always regretted that I did not have a brother. I did have a friend Jerry who was ten years older than me, and I always regarded him as my big brother. I met him when both of us were working for my cousin Bob and ultimately both of us became partners in Bob's different business ventures. Jerry did not realize just how funny some of his antics and malaprops were.

When I was twenty and working together with Jerry, we traveled to our factory in Pennsylvania one summer day in his flashy new De Soto. Jerry drove there and asked if I would like to drive back while he took a nap. The road was empty, Jerry snoozed, and I was flying, hitting 95 mph. He awoke, looked at his watch, and said we had made good time.

"How fast were you going?"

"About 65!", I fibbed.

I told my friend Brooks about my driving adventure, and he excitedly said that the next time we went, I had to go over 100 mph. We went again to Pennsylvania a month later and the same scenario occurred. Jerry slept and I went zipping through Pennsylvania, hitting 105 mph!

Driving through New Jersey, there was some construction on the highway ahead. A construction worker was waving a red flag to drivers next to a sign that said "Circle." There was a traffic circle and I went around it at 60 mph. Jerry went ballistic and screamed, "Didn't you see that sign, Circle?"

My answer was simple. I replied, " I thought it was the name of the town — Circle, New Jersey!"

The next day Jerry took his new car in for servicing because he said it was shaking.

I totally regret my reckless driving and to this day, I do not drive fast. In fact, some say that I drive like an old lady!

On another factory trip, Jerry and I drove through Allentown, Pennsylvania, home of Hess Brothers Department Store. Hess was the biggest store in the area, and it was really nice. We decided to stop and look around this famous store. I wandered into the men's department and started to try on some fashionable clothes. Jerry saw me wearing a beautiful gray sport jacket and asked me an important question. "How much money do you have in your pocket?"

When I answered that I had three dollars, I realized that I was about ninety-seven dollars short, so I returned the jacket, never to return to Allentown again!

***

Before Jerry got married, he and his friends rented a house in Ocean Beach, Fire Island, and I was often a weekend guest. His older friends liked me because I knew a lot of the younger girls at the beach and would always invite them to Jerry's house for a party. One night, we all went out to dinner at a local restaurant. Everybody ordered lobster and Jerry and I had never eaten a lobster before. One of his friends, Les was a joker and pulled a fast one on Jerry. The waitress had cleared Les's plate and Jerry asked him what happened to the lobster shell.

Les replied, " I ate it. It's the best part of the lobster."

Jerry started to chew on his lobster shell, and everyone at the table shook with laughter. Even Jerry laughed!

In later years, business was good and Jerry was taking a trip for the first time to Paris. He asked me to recommend the best things to see in Paris, and of course I told him about the fabulous Louvre Museum. When he came back, he gave me his reviews of Paris. He uttered this unbelievable quote, "THE LOUVER WAS SHIT!" I laughed for five minutes!

He then told me about the high prices in Paris. "Would you believe that I had a cup of coffee and a crouton for twenty-five dollars!"

He meant "croissant."

I responded, "Must have been one hell of a big crouton!"

***

Jerry was a big basketball fan and we often went to Knick games together. One night in the late 1970s, we were given great seats behind the Golden State Warriors bench. Golden State had a seven foot center, Clifford Ray, and Jerry with his loud voice was harassing this player all night. The game was close and with a few seconds to play, Jerry yelled, "Hey Clifford."

Clifford thought that the Warriors coach was calling him and he turned to face the bench. A pass meant for him went out of bounds, and the Knicks won the game by one point. Clifford was fuming but did not know who the culprit was. The Knicks should have given the game ball to Jerry!

One afternoon, Jerry, Bob, and I, and several others were sitting in my office having a sales meeting. My phone rang and the operator told me it was Robert Hall calling for Jerry. Robert Hall, a major customer of ours, was a big chain of stores selling inexpensive clothing to men and women. Jerry asked me who it was. Without cracking a smile, I told him, "It's Robert Hall. They say your new suit is ready to be picked up."

Everybody broke up laughing and the meeting was adjourned!

My friend Jerry was a cigar enthusiast, chewing rather than smoking, and always carried his supply of cigars in his briefcase. One day he told me that he had bought gold, on his broker's recommendation for being a good investment. He came to work the next day and told me how tired he was from schlepping his briefcase. Why was his briefcase so heavy? He opened it up and showed me thousands of dollars of gold coins! I guess he didn't trust the bank.

After chewing a cigar, Jerry would often deposit it into the closest ashtray. One afternoon, an elderly out-of-town buyer visited our office. When she saw what was in the ashtray, she remarked, "Where is the Great Dane?"

***

Jerry and I had lunch every day, usually at a dairy restaurant, R. Gross, where the food was terrific. When the restaurant was busy, people had to share a table. One lunchtime, we shared a table with two older gentleman who were discussing that night's baseball games.

"Who do you like, Toronto or Seattle? How about Houston or San Diego?", one man asked the other, in a thick European accent. Listening to the conversation, I asked how they could get excited about Toronto or Seattle, last place teams. The man responded, "Sonny boy, if you bet a thousand dollars on Toronto or Seattle, you would get excited too!"

I shut up and ate my gefilte fish.

Jerry left the business soon after I had left. We kept in touch, and after I moved to Florida and became a Certified Financial Planner, Jerry became a client of mine. Sadly, he got sick and passed away a few years ago.

***

I miss you Jerry. You were a good guy. You were the brother I never had!

MAN-TAN

A NEW PRODUCT CAME on the market in 1959 that was revolutionary, at least to me. I was a sun person, that is, I loved to sit in the sun to get a tan, usually with a sun reflector. Often I would go to "Tar Beach" (the roof of my apartment building). I was fair skinned, so I usually got red and sunburnt instead of getting a deep tan.

Dermatologists could have set up their office on the boardwalk at Bay 3 in Brighton. But now came the new product — Man-Tan!

When this lotion was applied to the skin, the user's pale skin was supposed to turn into a deep tan. What a great idea for the winter months! When I heard about this product, I ran to the drugstore to buy it. I applied it a few times and soon my skin color changed. But instead of a deep tan, I was turning deep orange!

After a day or two, the orange faded and I was moderately tan. When I picked up my Saturday night date, a young lady named Lee, she opened the door, and she was more orange than me!

Going back to school, friends asked me how did I get my tan. I told them that I was in Acapulco for the weekend.

GET ME TO THE CHURCH ON TIME

I HAD JUST TURNED twenty when I met a great looking girl, Cathy, very sophisticated and very mature. She was Italian, a non-practicing Catholic, and she told me that she was eighteen. A friend of my sister Arlene told her I was dating a non-Jewish girl. Needless to say, Arlene told this to my parents. My father would start singing whenever he saw me, "Get Me to the Church on Time," the great song from *My Fair Lady*.

Cathy invited me for lunch one afternoon at her house, and her mother asked me, "George, would you like a salami sandwich?"

I would never pass up a salami sandwich, so of course I said yes. My sheltered appetite only knew kosher salami but now I was eating Italian salami. I ate the sandwich, hated it, and to this day I do not eat Italian salami!

The winter day was unusually warm and I decided to be proactive and wax my father's Buick convertible in Cathy's driveway. I covered the car with blue Simonize wax which was easy to put on. When the sun went down and the temperature dropped about twenty degrees, the blue wax froze on the car and I could not get it off. My father's black and white Buick was now a blue Buick. Dad was not very happy with me!

My sister asked me if I knew how old Cathy was. I told her eighteen and she burst out laughing. Arlene said, "She's fifteen. Maybe she will invite you to her sweet sixteen party next year, when you'll be twenty-one."

Bye-bye Cathy!

***

Let's go forward just fifty-five years for the best part. I knew a woman Leslie who was an old friend of Cathy's and had told Cathy about me. Lo and behold, I get a phone call fifty-five years later from Cathy, asking me if I remembered her. I told her, "How could I forget you. Every time I hear "Get Me to the Church on Time," I think of you."

Catholic Cathy told me that fifty years ago, she had married a Jewish man whose parents insisted that she convert to Judaism. She had an Orthodox conversion and told me, "I am more Jewish than you!"

MIKE THE BARBER

IKE THE BARBER was truly a legend in Brooklyn in 1960. His tiny barbershop, not the cleanest, was located in a tough neighborhood about an hour from my home. His two dollar haircuts were the best in New York, as he was the first barber to cut hair with a straight razor. His shop was always crowded with all kinds of strange people — gamblers, bookmakers, loan sharks, etc. I was a college student and I stood out from the rest. Steve Lawrence, the popular singer, was a customer as were many minor celebrities.

To get an appointment, one had to call in advance to his payphone. If he said to come in at 7 p.m., that meant you would leave his shop at 11p.m. One night I actually left the shop at 1 a.m.

Everyone had a nickname — mine was "Georgie B" or George from Brighton. His appointment schedule was written on a piece of cardboard hanging next to the payphone on the wall.

One night he was excited. A friend of his had told Frank Sinatra, who was in New York, that Mike would give him the best haircut that he ever had. Mike had to leave the shop for a few minutes and and told everyone that if Sinatra called, to get the number and he would call him back. Needless to say, the phone rang and one of Mike's characters answered. The man jokingly told the caller, who indeed was probably Frank Sinatra, that Mike was out and had gone to the racetrack and he would not be back for a week.

When Mike returned and asked if anyone had called, the answerer said, "Some guy who said he was Sinatra, but I put him in his place."

Mike the Barber chased this character out of the shop and told him impolitely to never come back.

Bottom line, Frank Sinatra did not get the best haircut that he ever had!

THE BLIZZARD OF '61

IN FEBRUARY 1961, a big snowstorm hit the New York City area, burying it under a foot of snow. The snow was barely cleared when a week later, a second blizzard barraged the city, and Mayor Wagner decided to ban all nonessential traffic from the five boroughs.

That Saturday night I had a date, which was not unusual because I always had a date on Saturday night. Arlene M., great looking, was a first date for me, and I did not intend to break this appointment. Since I could not use my father's car, I decided to walk a few blocks to get the Ocean Avenue bus. Anticipating getting frostbite, I took a small bottle of Canadian Club whiskey with me and put it in the inside pocket of my parka. In the bitter cold, I trudged the few blocks to the bus stop, but alas, there was no bus and no taxis. I thought that perhaps I could hitch a ride to Avenue W, only a few miles away. I stood in the street utilizing my frostbitten thumb and soon a big Cadillac stopped for me. A man, his wife, and his daughter made room for me in the luxury car (I think this was my first Cadillac experience) and offered to drop me at Avenue W and Ocean Avenue. They were really nice people.

Now I had to walk seven blocks to East 27th Street through a foot of snow. Finally, an hour late, I reached my destination, rang the bell but was told that Arlene lived on East 26th Street. Again through the snow I trudged and finally found Arlene's house. Her mother took my coat and of course my whiskey bottle fell out. Mom wasn't too happy that her pride and joy daughter was going out with an alcoholic. I told her that the whiskey was for my frostbite, and she bought the story. We stayed in, watched television, and her mama fed me.

Soon it was midnight and time for me to leave. I trudged through the snow again hoping that the Ocean Avenue bus would be available. Of course it was not, again no taxis, and hardly any cars on the road. I was lucky the first time, so I figured that I would hitch a ride again.

A car stopped for me, and unbelievably it was the same Cadillac with the same three people. They insisted that they would take me to my door, and I was really appreciative. I think this was the first time that a Cadillac had ever been on Brighton 12th Street! To show my appreciation, I jotted down the daughter's name and phone number, and promised to call her for a date.

Unfortunately, a gust of wind blew the small piece of paper away, and it landed in a snow drift that was soon cleared away by a snow plow!

YOU'RE IN THE ARMY NOW

A YOUNG MAN ENTERING the Army in June 1961 should not have been as terrified as a young man might have been in 1941 after Pearl Harbor; in 1950 after the North Korean invasion; or in 1965 with the Vietnamese situation.

George Karp entered the Army in 1961 and he was scared!

I enlisted in the Army Reserves in April 1961, with my Army career well-planned. I would start two months of basic training in Fort Dix, New Jersey, that summer, followed by four months of training as a medic in Fort Sam Houston, in San Antonio, Texas.

I received a telegram in early June, basically telling me that I would be a soldier in one week. So much to do with so little time to do it!

That Friday afternoon, Bob and Jerry made me a surprise party in our office. All of my friends attended, as did some customers and I was really happy. That evening, I had a goodbye date with my longtime girlfriend Judy. Telling her that I was really tired, I left her to keep my midnight date with Barbara.

The next afternoon, my parents made me a surprise party at our apartment, and all my relatives were there. That night my friends made me a goodbye party at Brooks' house, that I think the whole world attended. I brought my date Margie to the party, and to top off a great two days, I got a speeding ticket!

The next morning, my father drove me to the bus station in Manhattan where I was to take a bus to Fort Dix, New Jersey. My father explained that I could not take my teddy bear with me, and I reluctantly agreed.

Fortunately (or unfortunately) for my dad, he had never served in the armed forces. He was too young to be in the First World War, and he was too old to be in World War II. I think that he was proud of me, proud that I was going to be a soldier.

I arrived at Fort Dix, got all my equipment and then I was officially a fighting man (even though I had never been in a fight, in my entire life)! Before I enlisted, a veteran friend of mine told me that when I arrive that first day, they will ask if anyone had taken ROTC in college. My friend advised that I should lie and tell them that I had ROTC experience because then I could become a squad leader and avoid KP (Kitchen Police). So, I told a fib and became a squad leader. However, I learned that lying to the Army was not a good thing to do.

Corporal Green, from Mississippi, saw right through me. He was amazed that I did not know how to march or follow commands. My only experience with a rifle was with a BB gun that I had when I was six. My first duty was to take apart and reassemble a rifle; I failed mightily. For every stupid detail that he handed out, he knew only one name — Karp.

At 4 a.m. one morning at reveille, an hour when I was usually getting home, it was announced that Corporal Green had been promoted to Sergeant Greene. Now I knew that with this promotion, I was in deep doodoo! I had a few options: I could run away; I could fake a nervous breakdown; I could consider an assassination. But as a mensch, I knew exactly what to do — I congratulated him!

Sergeant Greene was so excited since I was the only person to congratulate him that I became his best friend for the next two months. Now for the first time, he gave me the best details. We were buddies; he still calls me every week!

When it came time to get the official Army haircut, I was the last person in the barbershop. My friends came to see me one Sunday and they all laughed at my expense, when they viewed my very unfahionable crew cut.

On the schedule that was posted in the barracks, Thursday was listed as Activities Day. I was really happy because now I could play basketball, or baseball, or go swimming. Wrong! Activities day in the Army means painting the barracks, mowing the lawn, loading and unloading military vehicles, and other essential nonessential chores. I would have preferred basketball!

We got some time off one Saturday afternoon but with no pass to leave the base. I went to the Fort Dix swimming pool to relax a bit and saw a good-looking young lady. I started a conversation and ended up asking her out for that night. She laughed in my face and told me that she was a Lieutenant and she wouldn't be seen dead with a new recruit like me.

July Fourth fell on a Tuesday and for some reason, there was no Army work for Monday. A great holiday weekend, but we had no pass to leave the base. One of my Brooklyn associates had a great idea — let's go AWOL and go home. The plan was for Sunday: six of the Brooklyn boys would leave Fort Dix at 5 a.m., take a local taxi to Trenton, then take a Trenton taxi to Brooklyn. That evening, we would all meet fellow soldier Bill at his house, and he would take his car back to Fort Dix for bed check.

Everything went smoothly, and I was really excited to see the New York skyline at 6 a.m. However, the taxi driver told me, "I don't know how long you've been away…that's the skyline of Newark, New Jersey!"

When I came home, my parents were delighted to see me and made me a huge breakfast. I went to the beach, saw my friends, and had the best day. We all met Bill that evening, returned to Fort Dix, and left early the next morning — destination Brooklyn. Monday was the same as Sunday and that evening, we returned to Fort Dix. Tuesday was the carbon copy of Sunday and Monday, and for a short while, I felt like a civilian again!

The last week of basic training was the hardest — Bivouac Week meant that we were out in the field for the whole week. What really saved the day (actually the night) for me was the air mattress that I had smuggled in from the civilian world. It certainly beat sleeping on the cold, hard, and wet ground of old Fort Dix.

One night everyone had to hike a certain distance — far! One member of my squad had to read the compass, and of course, he read it wrong. We walked slowly through the biggest swamp in New Jersey, making friends with the alligators and snakes that were swimming past us. Finally, we came out of the swamp and walked for miles until we reached a road that I thought was the New Jersey Turnpike. An Army truck stopped for us and drove us back to our barracks where we were able to take a shower and take a nap, before we returned to the bivouac area. What a night!

I have many more boring stories about Fort Dix and basic training, but they won't be told.   After eight grueling weeks, in August 1961, I finally completed my basic training at Fort Dix. I felt good, I looked good, and I was in the best shape of my life. The Army gave me two weeks off for rest and relaxation, before I would go on to my next assignment. No, it was not armed combat in Vietnam, but rather three months of classroom medical study in Fort Sam Houston, in San Antonio, Texas.

America's fighting men — 1961.
Private Karp, in the middle of battle, in Basic training.

WAR IS HELL

W HEN I GOT off the plane in San Antonio, it felt like I was walking into an oven! Fort Sam Houston was considered the country club of the Army. There were many swimming pools for us to use; we could wear civilian clothes in the evening; and there were restaurants and clubs in San Antonio. Most importantly, only two hours away was Nuevo Laredo, Mexico, home of some great señoritas! My new friends and I went there every weekend, to foster better Mexican-American relations.

My platoon was made up of some of my basic training friends, mostly from New York, as well as a group of Philadelphia guys. There were people from all over the USA, and this gave me a chance to get to know what the rest of the country was like. The first day, I saw "Beetle" Bailey, a football player from Alabama, not having any soap, take a shower using a Brillo pad! Now I knew what Alabama was like — I'll take Brooklyn.

One Saturday night, a few Army friends and I, went to a very seedy club in downtown San Antonio. When we left around midnight, I noticed a big newsstand that was open and selling newspapers. In New York, I was accustomed to buying the Sunday New York Times late on a Saturday night. I asked the man if I could buy the Sunday Times and he told me, "Sure, come back on Wednesday!"

The Majestic Theater was the big movie theater in San Antonio. Around the corner, there was a big neon sign, "Majestic Colored Balcony." Years later, I unfortunately realized that this was the segregated South of 1961. I would have liked to have been there when that sign was torn down!

Realizing that we needed transportation, three of my new friends and myself chipped in and bought a car. We paid one hundred dollars for a 1949 Pontiac that had about 300,000 miles on the odometer. The tires were bald, the car was leaking oil, but at least we had a car. Over the years, this car must have had about fifty different owners, all local soldiers. Bottom line, we really never used it because it was too dangerous to drive, and when we left Fort Sam, we sold it back to the same used car dealer for seventy dollars! I'm sure that he quickly resold it for one hundred bucks to a new group of innocent soldiers.

Every day at about 5 p.m., all movement stopped at Fort Sam, and taps was played. There was no bugler, and a recording of taps was played on the record player near our barracks. One day, we were standing at attention in 100 degree heat, waiting impatiently to hear the taps recording. Suddenly, we heard Ray Charles singing "Hit the Road, Jack"! The culprit was never discovered (it was not me)!

***

In September and October, the Jewish holidays were observed and several of us discovered our Jewish roots. I think even a few Christians took advantage of the holidays and became Jewish for a few days. We stayed in San Antonio at a fancy hotel, about ten in our room, and actually went to Temple. Every few days, one of us would ask the Army Chaplain, "Any holidays this week?"

At a dance at the Temple, I met a pretty Jewish girl and asked her out. I explained that I had no car, and she said not to worry, she would pick me up at the base. She arrived driving a Cadillac convertible that was not too shabby! We had dinner at a local hamburger place that cost me about a dollar. She drove me around showing the sights of San Antonio, when another convertible pulled up alongside of us. There were six burly rednecks in the car who seemed to know my date. One shouted, "Hi, Jew Girl," and she waved and said, "Hi, Billy Joe."

I was furious with them and with my date for not getting angry. She explained that's what they called her in school and she accepted that. For sure, there was no second date!

Every two weeks, I was assigned KP (Kitchen Police), which meant being in the kitchen at 4 a.m. To get the best job, dining room orderly (DRO), one had to be in the kitchen by 2 a.m. Early one morning at 5 a.m., I was late, and I was assigned the worst duty, pots and pans. The cooks had made cherry pie in a huge vat, that I had to clean out. I had to climb up a ladder and then holding on, bend over and scrub out the vat. Trying to hold on, I lost my balance and was almost upside down, fearful of drowning in cherry pie. I was rescued and have not had any cherry pie since then!

The highlight of my Army career took place in the mess hall about two weeks later. On Fridays, fried fish was served for lunch, which really wasn't too bad. The Sergeant in charge of the kitchen told me to prepare the tartar sauce for the fried fish. He gave me a giant bottle of concentrated tartar sauce, told me to read the directions and add the right amount of water. I goofed — I misread the instructions and added way too much water. The tartar sauce became tartar soup! When the thousand soldiers came in for their lunch, tartar soup was not the best thing for their fried fish. The Sergeant was not too happy with me that day.

Finally, the time was coming (December 1) when I would be discharged from the Army. I couldn't wait to get out of there and reunite with my family and friends in Brooklyn. Thanksgiving was November 23 and the Army was planning a great feast for us, as opposed to the terrible dinners that had been served to us for the last three months. The commanding officer of Fort Sam, a General, was coming to our Thanksgiving turkey dinner. He arrived, we stood at attention, and he spoke to a few of us. He said to me, "Private Karp, what do you think of the food here at Fort Sam?"

I had to think quickly and had a choice of honestly saying that the food was terrible, or to lie and say the food was great. If I was honest, I would be looking at a week of KP or even worse. Discretion, being the better part of valor, made up my mind: "Sir, the meals here have been wonderful," I lied.

He loved hearing that and he shook my hand. I know I did the right thing and started to pack my bags for my return to Brooklyn. Considering that I was not headed to Vietnam but rather heading home to Brighton Beach, I felt lucky!

RUSSIAN SUBMARINES

IN THE EARLY 1960s, American young men faced a problem regarding the Armed Forces. With the Cold War with the Soviet Union in full swing, our government wanted to increase the American fighting force. A physically fit young man could do nothing, but then be subject to the military draft with an active duty service of two years. Or, he could enlist in the Army Reserves with different requirements: he would be on active duty for only six months but then be in the Army Reserves for five and one-half more years.

However, reserve duty entailed two weeks of summer camp at an Army post for five years, evening meetings once a week, and an all day Sunday meeting, usually once a month. Not being a conscientious objector and getting close to my college graduation, I was forced to make a quick choice about my future Army obligations. I chose the lesser of two evils — the Army Reserves.

As previously stated, I survived eight weeks of basic training in Fort Dix, New Jersey, and then spent four months in Fort Sam Houston, Texas, learning to be an Army medic. That's the background for this particular story.

I had an all day Sunday meeting scheduled for the first week in June at Fort Hamilton in Brooklyn. The Saturday night before, I had a date and got home very late, maybe 5 a.m. Getting up at 7 a.m. for the meeting, I was really beat, needless to say. Sunday was hot and sunny and the perfect beach day. I knew that all my friends would be at the beach, sunning and swimming, and I was very tired and very jealous.

The Army meeting was boring, the room was stifling, and I was dozing. I had to get out of there and I did. I left the armory, went to my car, and took out my old reliable shiny aluminum sun reflector. I couldn't leave Fort Hamilton, the Army post, so I found an old deserted building that would fit my needs. I took off my army jacket, my shirt and tie, and I got comfortable reclining against the wall, sun reflector in hand. The view was great, overlooking New York Harbor under the Verrazano Bridge. Immediately, I fell fast asleep.

Suddenly, I felt someone kicking my leg. Looking up, I gazed at the angry face of Major Sarcone, Commander of the Army unit. He growled, "What the hell are you doing here? And what the hell is that shiny thing?"

He confiscated my sun reflector and escorted me back to the armory.

After lunch, he called for a special formation of the five hundred reservists. Unbelievably, he bellowed, "We have a terrible situation here. This morning I discovered a soldier flashing signals with a shiny aluminum gadget to Russian submarines in New York harbor!"

Everyone knew that I was the culprit and the laughing was uncontrollable!

GEOGRAPHICALLY UNDESIRABLE

I WENT TO A friend's party in Manhattan during the winter of 1962. I met a nice lady Barbara from New Jersey, and we made a date for the following week. She lived in Paterson, which was quite a distance from Brighton Beach. Going there wasn't so bad, but coming home at 2 a.m. was the worst. To stay awake while driving, I had to open up all the windows, but it was about ten degrees outside. My nose was frozen! I had to drive for over an hour, and I decided not to do this again.

Barbara called me during the week, but I explained the ride home was terrible, so we had a problem. She told me that she liked me and her parents liked me, and her folks said it would be all right if I slept over. A date was arranged and I brought my best Batman pajamas.

I slept over and was sound asleep when I heard organ music playing. I figured that I was dead and this was my funeral with the organ playing. Fortunately, I woke up in a sweat and realized that I was still alive, and the music was coming from somewhere in the house. Barbara's father, who was not a funeral director, was playing the organ, probably to wake me up.

This whole situation was not for me. I had to tell Barbara that she was "GU" but she did not know what that meant.

I told her, "GU means Geographically Undesirable." Bye bye Barbara!

CLARENCE WAS NO ANGEL

CLARENCE WAS OUR shipping clerk when we started our business in 1962. He was not at all like his namesake, "Clarence the Angel" in the film *It's a Wonderful Life*.

At twenty-eight, he was a few years older than me, and even though our cultures were totally different, we became good friends. Besides being underpaid, Clarence had other problems. He told me that he was upset because his fourteen-year-old daughter, living in Mississippi, was pregnant.

Clarence was fourteen when this daughter was born, so the apple did not fall far from the proverbial tree.

Hypothetically, assuming that every generation had a child at age fourteen, then Clarence would be a:

1) grandfather at age 28
2) great grandfather at age 42
3) great great grandfather at age 56
4) great great great grandfather at age 70, etc.,etc.,etc.

Clarence had his problems, all right!

LIFE, LIBERTY &
THE PURSUIT OF HAPPINESS

SOON AFTER I began working for my cousin Bob in 1962, I really got to know Bob's partner, Frank. There was a famous actor at this time, Ernie Kovacs, who was an identical twin to Frank. Frank was a family man, devoted to his wife and children, but he had a girlfriend. He gave me a wonderful piece of advice. He said, "It's okay to cheat on your wife, but never ever cheat on your girlfriend!"

Frank knew a young man, Vinnie, who he thought would be an asset for the new business, and so he hired him. Vinnie and I were the same age, and we had a lot in common. I taught Vinnie about the sales aspect of our business and in time, we became very good friends. Vinnie had movie star looks and the girls loved him.

We went to Florida over the July 4th weekend, staying at the Fontainebleau Hotel in Miami Beach. Vinnie and I were the most popular people at the hotel and we met many, many girls. To say the least, we had a very good time!

Vinnie and I shared a room but there was one hangup. Vinnie told me that he could not sleep in a quiet dark room, so he gave me a choice:

a) sleep with the lights on

or

b) sleep with the television on.

I chose the television option, and I memorized the Declaration of Independence, because the television repeated it about 200 times that night!

TWO WEEKS IN ANOTHER TOWN

THE ADVANTAGE FOR my joining the Army Reserves was that I only had to spend six months on active duty. The disadvantage was that each summer for five years, I had to take my summer vacation from work and spend two weeks at an Army post.

There was a movie released in 1962, starring Kirk Douglas, called *Two Weeks in Another Town* that has nothing to do with my Army career, but it makes a nice title for this story.

My first summer vacation was spent at Fort Dix, New Jersey. Being a medic, I spent two weeks working in the Army hospital, having the very crucial job of putting talcum powder in rubber gloves, I assume to be used for prostate exams. With the Cold War in full swing, the U.S. Army was totally dependent on me and the rubber gloves project.

The Sergeant who was in charge of the talcum powder detail was a regular Army soldier who memorized the Army rulebook. He said to me, " Soldier, your hair is too long. Get an Army haircut immediately. I want to see white walls around your ears."

One of my fellow rubber glove workers Melvin defended me and whispered to the Sergeant, "Sarge, don't you recognize Private Karp? He is a television star and has to keep his hair long. If he gets a crew cut, he'll lose his job!"

The Sergeant understood my dilemma and asked me for my autograph!

I was prepared to go home for the weekend, but my favorite Sergeant recommended me for KP duty. Another wonderful Sergeant, probably his brother, was in charge of the kitchen and he and I got along famously. As I was washing out some pots and pans in lukewarm water, he became enraged. The Sergeant told me that to properly clean the pots and pans, I had to use really hot water. He turned on the water in the sink and it was scalding, maybe two hundred degrees. He roared, "Now that's the way you clean pots and pans — hot water!"

Not wanting to ruin my manicure, I told him, "Sergeant, you're right. But I'm a civilian and I am not going to stick my hands in boiling water. Sorry!"

Fortunately, he didn't speak to me again for the rest of the day.

***

I had to sleep in the barracks for two weeks and I was not happy. Some of the older guys had taken their cars and were sleeping in a motel in town. Several of my new Army friends and myself made a vow that the next summer we would rent hotel rooms and not sleep in the barracks.

In the spring, it was announced that our unit was going to Camp Drum in Watertown, New York, for our two-week tour of duty. One of my associates investigated Watertown and found the nicest hotel in town. We booked the honeymoon suite for the two weeks that we would be in Watertown. No barracks for this Brooklyn boy!

The time came and I went by bus to Watertown. About ten of us were going to sleep in the hotel for the two-week period. There were three different shifts of work:

8 a.m. to 4 p.m.; 4 p.m. to midnight; and midnight to 8 a.m. I got the day shift but two members of our group got the midnight shift.

Gene was a little fellow, but in his mind, he was a big ladies man. I explained to him that since he was off during the day, he had to make the connection with the girls staying at the hotel so that we could have a party every night. He loved his importance and got to know many of the chamber maids working at the hotel.

The second day there, Gene said to us, "Tonight we are having a party. I invited about six chamber maids to our suite at 8 o'clock."

Everyone was delighted, and we went out and bought food, beer, and vodka. The chamber maids, all dressed up and looking good, came to our hotel suite, and everyone ate and drank and had a VERY GOOD TIME! We planned to do this every night.

Gene had to go back to the post at midnight, and we warned him not to tell anyone about our party. He went back but could not resist telling some of the guys staying in the barracks. At 2 a.m., two of the barrack's boys came to our hotel room. We invited them in and they started to have one hell of a time. One of them, whose name was Jasper, worked for the sanitation department in Brooklyn. He got a little drunk and said to me something that I remembered for over fifty years. His was the classic line of all time:

"You Jews really can throw a party!"

THE CHOCOLATE SAUCE

SOMETIMES IN LIFE you learn a good lesson; other times, you learn that the lesson that you previously learned was not really a good lesson after all.

When I was a senior in college majoring in business, the head of the marketing department, a nice gentleman named Professor Eilbert, invited our whole marketing class to his home in Westchester. We had drinks there and then went out to a local restaurant for dinner.

Considering that I had about two dollars in my pocket, when the menu came, I ordered judiciously (judiciously is a favorite dish of mine). For two bucks, I could get a hamburger and a Coke and that's what I ordered. Some of my classmates stuffed themselves with roast beef and martinis — maybe they had a rich father. When the bill finally came, I was shocked to find out that the check was going to be shared equally. I was still hungry and had to borrow money to pay my share which was about fifteen dollars.

The lesson that I learned: when going out with a large group of people, one should order an expensive dish, because the bill was going to be shared equally.

About three years later, I was doing my two weeks active summer duty in Camp Drum in Watertown, New York. I was attached to the payroll section of my medical Army unit. We had just finished the tedious job of doing the payroll for the whole unit, and we decided to go out and celebrate at a nice restaurant. Not having been paid yet, I had about five dollars in my pocket, a big increase from three years ago. Remembering the experience with my schoolmates, now I ordered the roast beef and martini. Some of my army friends ordered big meals while others ate meagerly, and I felt sorry for the meager eaters because of the upcoming shared bill.

The check finally came and I waited for the shared bill. Much to my surprise, Ralph, the head of the unit who was a CPA in civilian life, took the bill. He pulled out his trusty Scripto lead pencil, that only CPAs used, and started to calculate. I knew then that I was in trouble because everyone was going to have to pay for what they ate, individually. I regretted ordering the roast beef and martini.

Ralph then uttered, "Who had the chocolate sauce?"

Again, I had to borrow some money from my friends to pay my share of the bill, which was about twenty dollars.

The lesson that I learned after two failed lessons was that one should not dine out with a group of people; one should dine alone.

Lesson learned!

THE CONCORD

THE CONCORD HOTEL, in Kiamesha Lake, New York, was a beautiful resort and the center of the famous "borscht belt." It was built in 1937 and lasted until 1998. I felt sad when I learned that the Concord was out of business.

In my single days of the early 1960s, my friends and I would go there often, and not as paying guests. We always had a good time! We had made plans to drive to the Concord the Sunday before Thanksgiving of 1963, to watch the Giants play the Cardinals. In those days, home games of the Giants were not locally televised and if one were a football fan, traveling out of New York was necessary to see the game.

That was the weekend of national tragedy — President Kennedy was assassinated that Friday, November 23, 1963. The NFL refused to postpone Sunday's games, which I felt was a poor decision. My friends Brooks, George, and I thought that we would all feel better if we spent the day at the Concord, watching football and maybe meeting some girls.

We did meet some girls who invited us to their room, while they called room service. We had a huge Concord lunch that was really great. That afternoon, we hung around the big Concord bar, watching the game, sipping a Pepsi. (It was really not a Pepsi!).

Suddenly, a girl that we knew came running into the bar, shouting, "Some Jew just shot Lee Harvey Oswald in Dallas."

"Impossible," I said, "There are no Jews in Dallas."

I certainly was wrong. On National television, Jack Ruby killed Lee

Harvey Oswald on a day that I and the rest of the country will never forget.

***

A few years later, Kathy and I were on our way to the Concord, for a December mini-vacation. My car was in for servicing, so I had to rent a car for the weekend, a white Chevy. It was raining when we left New York City, and as we got closer to our destination, the rain turned to snow. Very soon, we were in a blizzard, and when we finally reached the Concord, the snow was really coming down and was deep.

We had a fun weekend and then it was time to go home. It had stopped snowing, but the snow on the ground was really high, maybe twenty inches or so. Everyone was checking out at the same time, and there was a huge line for the bellhops to retrieve cars. It didn't make sense to wait hours for the bellhop, so I decided to get my car myself.

That was a bit of a mistake! The parking lot was gigantic and hundreds of cars were buried under the snow. I went up and down the aisles looking for my rented car, and I didn't even know what it looked like. I had to brush away the snow from each license plate to see if that was my car. Finally, I found it, and with frost bitten hands and frost bitten feet, we headed home!

***

During the summer, around 1979, we took the kids who were home from camp, to the Concord for a few days. One evening, Kathy and I went to the nightclub to see the show. There were long tables, and we sat with strangers, awaiting the show.

As you probably realize, I have a pretty good memory and I remember places, and faces, and names. The woman sitting across from me looked very familiar, and I quickly remembered who she was. I said to her, "I think I know who you are. Your name is Judy, you were in my class in the second grade at P.S. 254, and you lived on Ocean Avenue."

She looked at me in disbelief. I told her my name and she had no idea who I was. She could not believe that I recognized her. I think she had told the man that she was with, who was not her husband, that she was ten years younger than she really was. She was getting really nervous that I would start discussing years and age, and they quickly changed tables.

Bye-bye Judy — see you in another forty years!

HOW I MET MY WIFE

P EOPLE ALWAYS ASK me, "How did you meet your wife?"
Since I have had two wives, I have two answers for them.

I met Kathy (wife number 1) under strange conditions. My friend Brooks and I had a great understanding. Whenever I started dating a new girl, I always asked her if she had any good-looking friends I could introduce to my friends. Brooks would do the same thing for me. In December 1963, he was dating a nice girl who lived in Manhattan, and he arranged a blind date for me one Saturday night. I always judged a book by its cover and in this case, I was not crazy about the cover. Maybe the book was better than the cover, but fortunately for everyone, I never got the chance to read the book — not even page one!

As always, we went out after 9 p.m., so that cleverly, we did not have to take the ladies out for dinner. That night, we went to the cocktail lounge at the Carlyle Hotel, that was famous because the Kennedys used to stay there. My friend George R. met us there with his date. Not being enamored with my blind date, my eyes wandered around the room. Across the room from where I was sitting, I spotted a great-looking girl.

After a while of making eye contact, she got up to go to the ladies room. I excused myself from my table and followed her out. After fifteen minutes of waiting, I figured that she had stomach trouble, so I gave up and went back to my table. The mystery lady finally came out and we continued to eye each other. Then, she and her date got up to leave, and I figured that was the end of the story. But, as the lady passed my table, she tossed something to me, landing in my lap. It was a rose with a card that had her name and phone number on it. My friends both said that it was for them and she had bad aim! I called her the next day and the rest, of course, is history.

There are so many "what if's" here. What if:

 a) I was busy that night having another date

b) I liked my blind date and I was not looking around the room

c) I was sitting in another seat at the table and was not facing Kathy

d) We did not go to the Carlyle Hotel, etc.

If any of this was so, then my children and grandchildren would not be reading this book because they wouldn't exist!

***

I met Rita (wife number 2) under a more normal set of circumstances. I moved to Boca Raton in 1992 and began to socialize as a single man. I hadn't met anyone special, and I was starting to get bored. In July 1993, I saw an ad in *the Sun-Sentinel* saying that there would be a singles party at the JCC that Saturday night. Not having plans, I decided to go by myself. I had a premonition that tonight would be special, and I would meet someone special.

I think that the Sun-Sentinel is read almost exclusively by women. At the party, there were about 200 ladies and including me, only three men. The other two men were creepy, and it looked like I had cornered the market on single women. I wandered about, scouting the scene, judging plenty of books. I certainly had my choice of ladies, and there in the corner, talking to her friend, sat great-looking Rita.

I introduced myself, spoke at length, and took her phone number. As with wife number one, I called her the next day and again, the rest is history.

Thank you, *Sun-Sentinel*!

KATHY'S CLOWN

FIRST MAN ASKS second man, "How long have you been married?" Second man answers, "I've been a happily married man for three years. But, I've been married for twenty years!"

Kathy and I were happily married for twenty-six years — out of twenty-seven years. But people change and life must go on.

I've already explained how Kathy and I first met. After a few dates, Kathy was going to prepare a dinner for me, and she asked what was my favorite dish. I told her that I loved duck, and she made me a fabulous duck dinner. I thought, Wow, this girl can cook! Many years later, she confessed that the duck dinner came from Casserole Kitchen!

Early in our relationship, Kathy wanted to introduce me to some of her relatives, so we went to dinner at the home of an old aunt and uncle in Queens. The uncle had a very thick European accent and I could barely understand him. He was telling me about his son who was a professor at Howard University. I told him that I had heard of Howard and that it was a fine black college. The aunt quickly jumped in and said, "No, he teaches at Harvard, not Howard."

I was embarrassed and couldn't wait for dinner!

The next week we went to dinner with another aunt and uncle, in a fancy building in Manhattan. These relatives were wealthy and had a very big, modern art collection. I viewed the paintings and sculptures and was truly impressed. One of the modern sculptures was a big piece of charred wood. Trying to be funny, I said to the aunt, "Must have been one heck of a fire."

She didn't laugh and didn't talk to me the rest of the evening!

***

I was just a poor Jewish boy from Brooklyn, trying to impress Kathy, a wealthy Jewish girl from Manhattan. On a Saturday evening in 1964, we went out on a date and tried a trendy restaurant, Gatsby's, on First Avenue. I had never heard of American Express or Diners Card, so I had to rely on the fifteen dollars in cash that I had in my pocket.

Knowing that I was on a budget, I ordered sparingly (a hamburger) while Kathy had a steak. I left hungry but within my fifteen dollar budget. I had given my car to the parking attendant outside, but I did not have a dollar for a tip. Fortunately, I had some change in my raincoat pocket, maybe forty cents, including pennies, and I handed it to the attendant when he brought my car around.

He examined the meager tip, handed it back to me, and said, "Here, you need this more than me!"

That was the last time I went to Gatsby's!

***

A few years later, after Jennifer was born, Kathy and I traveled to Mexico and stopped in a small town between Mexico City and Acapulco. We were on a tour and had no say about where we would spend the night. We stayed at a dilapidated old hotel that had no air conditioning and certainly no room service. This was a "minus five-star" hotel. There were gaping holes in the wall and all sorts of Mexican bugs could fly in. At 4 a.m., in the bathroom, I saw two tarantulas doing the mambo!

There were wild dogs and wolves outside howling and I called this memorable night, "The revolt of the dogs!"

***

In the early 1970s, Kathy and I went to see the Giants play at Yankee Stadium. We met her obstetrician, Dr. Dubrow, who had delivered our three children. He didn't seem to remember her face, but I told her that he might remember other parts of her body!

One Saturday night, we went out to dinner in the city and I parked in the garage of the new General Motors building. Waiting for my car, I noticed that the monthly rate for parking was ninety dollars. I said to

Kathy that ninety dollars was more than the rent we paid in Brighton. Kathy asked, "For your car?"

"No", I replied, "Rent for our apartment!"

I always took pride in my humor and there were people that I liked because they always laughed at my jokes. Kathy's mother Peggy was my best audience. I tried very hard to get Kathy to laugh at me but to no avail. One day, I had my toolbox out and had to hammer a nail into the wall. Unfortunately, I hammered my thumb, and finally Kathy laughed hysterically. My thumb still hurts and Kathy is still laughing!

In the early 1980s, Kathy went to Florida to visit her mother for the weekend. The plan was for me to pick her up at LaGuardia Airport when she returned that evening. Still trying to make her laugh, I had an idea. I found my old, red hooded sweatshirt and a pair of Bermuda shorts to wear, even though it was twenty degrees outside. I drove to the airport, parked, and waited for my wife. I put up the hood of the sweatshirt, tied it very tightly, so that my ears were sticking out. I must say that I looked like an idiot!

Finally, my elegant wife appeared, wearing a mink coat. When she saw me, she almost fainted, and she walked past me resembling a speed walker. Needless to say, I did not make her laugh!

***

After my short retirement, we took a trip in 1984 to California, traveling from south to north. San Francisco was bustling because of the Democratic National Convention. When I booked the trip, I did not realize that the convention was going on, and I could not get a room in a hotel that I really wanted. I was able to get a reservation in a hotel that was not quite a five-star hotel, but rather a zero-star hotel. To say the least, my wife was not pleased with my choice and threatened physical violence if the hotel was not changed. I called a nice hotel, and was able to book a room because of a cancellation. As I was checking in, I noticed Kathy was smiling and had made small talk with a man who had just left the lobby. Angrily, I asked her just who was she talking to?

She replied, "Oh, nobody important. Just President Jimmy Carter!"

The next winter, we went to Tucson and stayed at the Canyon Ranch. The first morning there, I wanted to take a hike in the mountains with a group of people. Kathy was tired and did not want to go. The walkers and I hiked for about an hour in the mountains and then tired and hungry, we came back. Always a joker, I told the group of twenty that I wanted to introduce them to my wife who was waiting in our room. Sleeping Kathy was not very happy when I paraded twenty sweaty people into our tiny room!

The next day, she went on the hike.

***

Heather and Vanessa went to summer school at Wellesley College in Boston, and Kathy and I went to visit them one weekend in 1986. Boston is a great city and we started our little tour on the subway, the "T". Somehow, Kathy and I got separated on the train and I tried to find her. It was a comedy of errors, and there is a song about the Boston subway, "the MTA," about a man who could not get off the train. I think that song was written about us. Finally, we reunited!

Another "lost" incident happened in Russia. In 1987, on our trip to the Soviet Union, our tour bus took us for a viewing of a large park in Moscow. Kathy wandered about and got separated from the rest of our group. I could not find her. Considering that she had no money, could not speak Russian, and did not even know the name of the hotel where we were staying — she had a problem. I convinced the bus driver not to leave until we came back and somehow he agreed. The park was huge, but I was lucky and found her.

Everybody cheered when Kathy got on the bus!

ANOTHER OPENING, ANOTHER SHOW

OPENING NIGHT ON Broadway used to be a big deal. Celebrities appeared on the red carpet outside the theater and everyone dressed formally.

In 1964, a new show, *The Sign in Sidney Brustein's Window* opened and was destined to be a big hit. The play was written by Lorraine Hansberry, author of *Raisin in the Sun*. In those days, opening nights would start earlier than usual because the newspapers wanted to make sure that their reviews would be in time for the morning papers. Also, the television networks wanted to have their reviews on the 11 o'clock news.

Somehow, Kathy had secured tickets for opening night. I was wearing my tuxedo and Kathy was wearing a gown, and we were in the theater, mingling with celebrities. When the show was over, we went outside where people were being interviewed by CBS news. Waiting my turn to be interviewed, I thought of some clever things that I would say to the reporter. Kathy and I both were interviewed along with about 100 other people. We went to a friend's apartment to watch the news, and somehow I had the premonition that my little speech would be used.

I called my parents in Brooklyn, waking them up and telling them to watch CBS news. Lo and behold, there I was on television — a theater critic. I figured that so many people had seen me that I was now a minor celebrity. Going to work the next morning, the elevator operator (does anyone know what an elevator operator is?) in my building said that he had seen me on the news. Now I figured that the whole city had seen me and I would be getting hundreds of phone calls that morning. I sat by the phone all day but the phone never rang.

I guess everyone had watched the news on NBC!

INSURANCE SCAM

I FINALLY GOT MY first car, a 1964 Pontiac Catalina convertible (Marimba Red), and I was thrilled! This baby had air-conditioning even though air-conditioning in a car then was really exclusive.

I parked my shiny new car in the garage of my apartment building, and as I was slowly driving up the ramp to the street, a young boy on a bicycle ran right into the side of my car. I wasn't going fast and he wasn't going fast, but he got knocked off the bike and was crying. It didn't look like he was hurt, but some neighbors took him to his apartment.

My Marimba Red new car was not even scratched.

The accident clearly was not my fault, but I felt badly for the kid, and so that evening I went to pay him a visit. Before I rang the bell, I heard the injured child laughing, singing and running around. When I rang the bell and told the mother who I was, I heard her screaming to her son, "Arnold, get into bed, quick!"

She let me in and I saw little Arnold in his bed, making believe that he was hurt. I knew that he was faking and that he was really fine.

Arnold's family sued my insurance company, and they probably collected a great deal of money because Arnold's mother was now driving the only Rolls-Royce in Brighton Beach!

BOB'S BIG BOY

IN CALIFORNIA THERE is a restaurant chain called Bob's Big Boy. Every time I pass this restaurant, I think of my first cousin Bob's big boy son, Howard. I guess Howard would be considered my first cousin, once removed, whatever that means.

Bob was not a big baseball fan but his son Howard was, and certainly I was the number one fan in New York. Bob had bought two tickets for the Saturday game of the 1964 World Series but he did not want to go. He asked me if I would like to take his twelve-year-old son to the game. Even though I hated the Yankees, I had never been to a World Series game before, so I would gladly go and root for the Cardinals.

Yankee Stadium was packed and we saw a great game. Actually I saw a great game; Howard spent most of the game at the hot dog stand. He even found a twenty dollar bill which he did not share with me. The game was tied 1-1 in the ninth inning and Mickey Mantle was up first. The stadium was clouded with cigar smoke (yes, in those days, cigar smoking was allowed at the ballpark), and we could barely see home plate from our distant seats in left field. I told Howard, "Let's go, Mantle is going to hit a home run and end the game."

Of course Mickey did, and we beat the crowd out of the ballpark. Howard thought that I was a genius!

Young Howard's bar mitzvah was a comedy of errors. The services that Saturday morning were being held in Forest Hills, Queens. I knew that there was a big synagogue on Queens Boulevard, and we got there just a little late. Kathy and I sat in the back of the big room and I looked around for people that I knew. Not recognizing anyone, I realized that something was amiss when they called the bar mitzvah boy to the podium, and unless Howard had gained about one hundred pounds, I knew that we were in the wrong synagogue!

Asking directions, I found the right synagogue and arrived just as the service was ending. I told Howard that his reading was just terrific, and he should consider becoming a Rabbi!

***

About fifteen years later, Howard came to work for our company. One day for lunch, he ordered a big, rare roast beef sandwich from Jimmy's, a great restaurant near our building. As he was chomping on his huge sandwich, my back was towards him, and I was opening the big safe that we had in the office. I asked him a question and instead of him answering me, I heard a squeaking noise.

I turned around and saw that his face was purple, and he could not talk or breathe. Realizing that he was in big trouble, I knew that I had to apply the Heimlich maneuver on him. My kids had learned the maneuver in school and had practiced for weeks on me. With my fingers extended, I hit Howard once and then again in his solar plexus.

A two pound wedge of rare roast beef came flying out of his mouth and bounced along the floor like a hockey puck. Just then, Pearl, our bookkeeper, walked into the room and screamed because she thought the rolling roast beef was a mouse!

Howard told me that he was black and blue for weeks, but he was indebted to me because I had saved his life!

When I retired from the company in 1984, Howard told me that he missed me and sadly admitted that all the humor was now gone from the office!

MY THREE DAUGHTERS

THE GREATEST MEMORY a man can have is the memory of his child being born. Therefore, I have three great memories!

My first daughter Jennifer was born in June 1967, on the third day of Israel's victorious Six-Day War. The fact that tiny Jennifer, when I first saw her, resembled a baby chicken, could not diminish the unbelievably happy feeling that I felt. Chicken Little grew to be a beautiful child and then to a beautiful woman.

Kathy's first remark to me was, "How does my hair look? I had it done today."

I raced home from Lenox Hill Hospital in Manhattan to Fort Lee to attempt to assemble Jennifer's crib. After four hours, sweating, I completed my task, only to realize that I had done it wrong and had to do it all over again.

The next day in the hospital, they allowed me to feed Jennifer. Nervous and sweating profusely, I was concerned that I was not feeding her correctly. The nurse told me that I was doing a fine job and Jennifer would not be undernourished.

***

Heather, my second daughter, was born three years later. I had basketball tickets that night to see the Knicks play the Baltimore Bullets (now the Washington Wizards) for the division championship. I gave my ticket away and headed to Lenox Hill Hospital, awaiting the birth.

Dr. Dubrow, a basketball fan, told me that it would be hours until the baby was to be born. He suggested that I go to his apartment to watch the game and that he would call me when something was happening. Kathy insisted that I go, so I went to his apartment where his wife made dinner for me, and we watched the game together. The Knicks won the game and I quickly headed to the hospital just as the baby was born. I was so happy!

If the baby was a boy, I thought of naming him either "Willis Reed Karp" or "Walt Frazier Karp," in honor of the Knicks' victory!

***

Three years later, in 1973, my third daughter was born. She was a tiny redhead and a ball of fire already. We did not have a name for her, and the hospital staff told us that she could not go home until she was named. The name "Baby Karp" was not acceptable to the hospital. We deliberated and every time we thought we had a name selected, both Jennifer and Heather said, "Oh no, we hate that name."

Finally, everyone agreed on the name Vanessa. Now with three terrific daughters, my family was complete!

Jennifer graduating nursery school in 1972;

Columbia graduate school in 2005.

YANKEE DOODLE

J OE PEPITONE PLAYED first base for the New York Yankees in 1967. Joe was a good hitter, could have been a great hitter, but I think that he was his own worst enemy. He played in the major leagues for twelve years and had quite a few productive seasons.

Kathy and I moved to Fort Lee that year, into a big apartment house, Mediterranean Towers. Joe lived there also with his wife and baby daughter.

One evening, Kathy went food shopping and I watched baby Jennifer. Joe was in the lobby talking to the doorman when he saw a good-looking lady, struggling with her groceries. He didn't know Kathy and asked her if she needed help with the bags. She told him yes and he carried the bags upstairs for her, maybe with something else on his mind besides eggs and milk.

After they knocked, I opened the door for them and Joe was visibly disappointed when he saw me. I thanked him, and I was tempted to give him a twenty-five cent tip, but I realized that he was making a huge salary from the Yankees, so I just shook his hand and got his autograph!

COME THE REVOLUTION

THE YEAR 1968 was one of the worst years in the history of our country. Two assassinations shocked the nation — first Martin Luther King, Jr. and then Robert F. Kennedy.

The war in Vietnam was escalating, and there was tremendous opposition in the United States to this unpopular war. Young people opposing Government policies, rioted at the Democratic National Convention in Chicago, causing many deaths and injuries.

Times were indeed bad!

One morning, I was in a taxi going to see a customer in downtown Manhattan (Uber was still forty years from being created). I was neatly dressed, wearing a suit with a shirt and tie. I started a conversation with my young taxi driver, who was not wearing a suit and tie, but proudly displayed a tattoo on his burly forearm. He was an angry young man, talking about the injustices in our country and especially about the war in Vietnam.

Unbelievably, he growled at me, "When the revolution starts, we're going to get people like you!"

"*Me?*", I responded nervously, sounding like Woody Allen. "I'm just a nice Jewish boy from Brooklyn. I'm wearing a suit because my mother dressed me this morning. I hate the Vietnam War, I hate the Democrats and hate the Republicans, and love the Cubans, the Russians, and the PLO."

I figured I had to touch all the right bases.

I wonder whatever became of that revolutionary taxi driver.

Possibly after the revolution, he went to work for Goldman Sachs!

THE KEY, THE KEY!

WHEN JENNIFER WAS about two years old, we hired a babysitter for her. Mary Alice, age fourteen, was a quiet, bright young girl, but she would not qualify for the Miss Teen America Beauty contest. She babysat every Saturday night, and Kathy and I had a set routine at the end of the evening. I double parked outside our building, Kathy went upstairs, and Mary Alice came down to the car to give me the house key. (Keys were expensive and we only had one key!) Then I drove her home.

On this Saturday night, Mary Alice came down to my car and got in. I held out my hand so that she could give me the key and she looked at me kind of funny. She took my hand and held it. "The key, the key!" I screamed, "Give me the key!"

I don't know if she was embarrassed or disappointed, but I drove her home.

The next week we had a new routine — I went upstairs, Kathy waited downstairs, and Kathy drove her home!

I CAN'T KICK!

A NEW FRIEND OF mine Chuck, lived in the same building in Fort Lee as I did, and he had season tickets to all the Knicks' games. He did some dry cleaning work for the Knicks, and he was very close to the team management and the players. He knew that I loved basketball, so he invited me to a game and I readily accepted. The seats weren't bad, only first row, midcourt.

In 1969, the Knicks had a star player Cazzie Russell, who had broken his ankle a few weeks before. Obviously, he could not play for a while, and he sat next to me, with a big cast on his foot. Many people approached him and asked him the same question: "Cazzie, how's your foot?"

He gave everyone the same answer, which is a classic, — "I can't kick!"

I loved that line!

After the game, I waited for Chuck while he collected the sweaty Knick uniforms and put them in his car. We drove home and instead of having the expensive satin uniforms dry cleaned, he tossed them into the building's washing machine. "They come out better being washed," he said.

Somehow, I didn't quite believe him!

TWILIGHT OF A MEDIOCRE CAREER

TENNIS WAS, AND still is, one of the great pleasures of my life. I've been playing for a very long time, and now I can say that I am in the twilight of a mediocre career! (Actually, that is a quote from a funny baseball player, Frank Sullivan, and I regard it as a classic!)

I started to play tennis in 1969 at the outdoor courts of my building in Fort Lee, New Jersey.

I was playing (or trying to play) one day with a friend Mike, and I was having a hard time serving. I asked Mike if I could just throw the ball in, instead of serving it in! Of course, he said, "No." And then, I aced him — I wish!

Don, a neighbor was painfully watching the match, and when it was finally over, he gave me some sound advice — "Play golf!"

Twenty years later, a funny incident occurred at East River Tennis, where I was a member for many years. I was playing on a Saturday morning from 10 a.m to 11a.m. Just before 11, I noticed that many people were standing behind the court, watching my game. This was not exactly the finals at Wimbledon, and I did not know why so many people were interested in watching four old guys double fault.

As I picked up a ball in the corner of my court, a player on the next court was picking up a ball in the corner of his court. We looked at each other — I recognized him, and then I realized why so many people were standing behind the court.

They were not there to see George Karp, they were there to see Robert Redford!

A DAY AT THE BEACH

I T WAS A beautiful July Friday in 1969. I took the day off from work, and along with some neighbors from Fort Lee, we went to Jones Beach on Long Island. I think this was the first time that two-year-old Jennifer had seen the ocean and she loved it.

It was hot and I went into the ocean by myself. I saw a young girl struggling in the water. It looked like she needed help, and being a good Samaritan, I volunteered to help her. I took her hand and tried to take her to the shore, when she suddenly grabbed me around the neck, pulling me underwater.

I released her grasp and surfaced, and saw that she was laughing at me, along with her friends. No more Mr. Nice Guy!

The best part of the day came when I had to make a phone call to my office. Our operator told me that the buyer from Lerner Shops had called for me. From a pay phone (remember what a payphone was?) on the boardwalk, I called the buyer, and she gave me the biggest order of the season!

Figuring that Jones Beach was my lucky charm, I took the next Friday off, and we went to Jones Beach again. Not only did it rain, but when I called my office, I found that Kmart had given me a big cancellation.

Disregarding Jones Beach the next Friday, I went to work!

THE WATER HOSE CAPER

I MUST SAY THAT this story is really unbelievable.

It was the winter of 1970 and I was on my way home from work in Manhattan, heading to Fort Lee, New Jersey. I was driving my new Buick Electra on the East River Drive (now the FDR Drive). I was near East 100th Street when my new car started to sputter and finally stopped. I tried to start it but I could not. Traffic was stalled, and the driver of the car in back of me got out of his car and told me that he would push me to the next exit, 110th Street. Since that was my only choice, I told him, "Yes, but please be careful."

Slowly, he pushed me to the exit, and I was able to park on a dark street in a very bad neighborhood. What the heck was I going to do? If I only had a cell phone, I could call AAA, but cell phones were still twenty years away from being invented!

That day at work, a customer had paid me some money, in cash, that he had owed the company. But, it was too late to go to the bank, so I put the cash in my pocket. Now here I was in a bad neighborhood with a lot of cash, and I was nervous. Using my great intellect, I put the money into my shoe — just in case. I would not be robbed of that money — maybe murdered, but not robbed!

A man passing by told me that there was a gas station about two blocks away, and I started to walk there, or rather, limp there. I found the gas station but this was not the shiny Exxon station shown on television — it was seedy! It was guarded by a giant ferocious German Shepherd on a thick chain. The proprietor, looking like he was just released from Sing Sing prison, told me that he and his boys would push my car the two blocks to his gas station. They did this and after examining the engine, they told me that my water hose was broken and would have to be replaced.

The only problem was that they did not have a replacement water hose. The boss said, "Don't worry man, we'll get you one."

"From where?" I innocently asked.

"Don't worry, man, we'll steal one from another car in the street," he replied.

About an hour later, the men returned with a "hot" water hose. They installed it and I did not ask about a warranty. Still limping, I asked the boss how much I owed him.

"How much you got?" he demanded.

I emptied out my pockets to show that I had a roll of quarters, five dollars worth for the washing machine in my building, and two single dollar bills. My new friends were disappointed but quickly took all the money. I think they felt sorry for me because of my bad leg which I told them was from when I was wounded in Vietnam.

I asked to use their phone that was guarded by the giant dog, and I limped over to use it, while the dog was snarling. I think he smelled the money in my shoe!

When I finally got home, Kathy asked if I had a nice day.

"Oh yes, peaceful and relaxing," I lied.

IF IT'S TUESDAY, THIS MUST BE
BROOKLYN

*I*F *IT'S TUESDAY, This Must Be Belgium* is an old movie from the '60s, that tells of a whirlwind tour through Europe in just a few days. Along with our friends, Lenny and Sue, Kathy and I replicated the movie in 1972. This was my first trip to Europe and I loved it. We visited Barcelona, Madrid, Rome, Paris, Nice, Lisbon, and many other cities in just a handful of days.

In Madrid, we had a few funny experiences. I was just starting to play tennis at home and I was anxious to play in Europe, so I brought my tennis racket (wood) with me. I asked the concierge where I could play tennis, and he told me that there was a park a few blocks away.

The only thing was that players had to supply their own net, and he could sell me a net for only one hundred fifty dollars! Gracias, but no thanks!

We made reservations in advance at Madrid's finest restaurant. The silverware was gold, so I guess you could call it "goldware." Across the room sat Rex Harrison, the English movie star, with three great-looking women. He was really drunk and was making a lot of noise, and he actually had to be carried out of the restaurant.

Our friends wanted to go to a disco that they had heard about. We left the restaurant and told the doorman the name and address of the disco, and with difficulty he hailed a cab (No Uber yet). He gave the driver directions in Spanish. The taxi turned the corner and thirty seconds later stopped in front of the disco. Who opened the door for us

— none other than the doorman of the restaurant! We all had a great laugh, as I tipped him the second time!

***

We arrived in Rome on Ascension Day, a major Catholic holiday. We were in St. Peter's Square along with about two million screaming Italians, when the Pope appeared on his balcony, about three miles away. He waved to me and I waved back, so I guess I can say that I had an audience with the Pope!

The hotel in Nice was nice. Kathy went out on our balcony, overlooking the street, and started to scream. Why was she screaming?

"The Louis Vuitton store is just across the street," she excitedly said.

"Big deal," I answered!

We rented a car and I thought that I would be the driver. I couldn't understand why the car had three pedals. Lenny explained that the third pedal was the clutch, whatever that was. Lenny became the driver, thank goodness, and as he flew across the Grand Corniche, my eyes were tightly closed. I don't know if I could have driven with my eyes closed. My first European trip was really great!

***

About ten years later, we traveled to the Acapulco Princess with Lenny and Sue. My cousin Bob was at the hotel the week before, and he had made all kinds of reservations for us. I did not know the meaning of the word "dermatologist" then, and I loved to sit in the sun with my sun reflector. Bob gave me strict instructions on how to reserve lounges by the pool.

He said, "As soon as you get to the hotel, go to the pool and ask for Pablo, *the pool director*. Tell Pablo who you are and that you are friends of Senor Bob, and you want four lounges under a tree for the next week. Also, both of you give Pablo fifty bucks."

We met Pablo at the pool, slipped him fifty dollars apiece, and told him what we wanted. He said, "Si, Senor," but I sensed he was not an English scholar. The next morning when we went down to the pool, we noticed that our lounges were occupied. When I asked the lifeguard for Pablo, the pool director, he laughed and pointed me to the kiddie pool. Pablo, the pool director, was scrubbing the kiddie pool on his hands and knees, and when I asked him about the lounges, he smiled and said, "Si, Senor!"

**

A few days later, we went deep-sea fishing in Acapulco Bay. Enduring the rough seas after a few hours, I hooked one and the crew helped me bring the huge sailfish onto the boat. I was pleased with my accomplishment and decided to throw the fish back in the water. The captain said, "Oh no, Senor. This is the biggest sailfish that we have ever caught. You must have it stuffed."

Reluctantly, I agreed and paid a lot of money for stuffing my record fish. Finally, they shipped it to New York, and I realized that it was made of plaster and paint. This was a classic Mexican rip-off!

The next winter we traveled to St. Martin and stayed at the newest hotel, La Samana. Our room was beautiful, but unfortunately we had to share it with another — a mouse. We had gone out to dinner the first night, and I left a candy bar on the counter. Our new roommate, Mickey, had eaten half of my Hershey bar, without thanking me. Lenny got a broom, spotted the rodent, and chased it out of the room. That's it for St. Martin!

**

Back in New York, we were having dinner with Lenny and Sue one evening, and the tables were very close together. It was winter and one of the men sitting next to us was wearing a beautiful white flannel suit. I was drinking red wine out of a long stemmed glass when my finger accidentally tipped over the glass, and the red wine cascaded toward the other table. It was like slow motion, and I saw this flow of red wine land in the lap of the man in the white flannel suit. I didn't know what to do, but the man said that it was no problem. Although the suit was probably ruined, I offered to pay the cleaning bill, but the man flatly refused my offer.

That was the last time I had red wine — white wine is safer!

THE INCREDIBLE SHRINKING COAT

As previously stated, the first European city that I had ever been to was Barcelona, in the spring of 1972. There was just so much to see and we loved it. Our friends, Lenny and Sue, wanted to go shopping and of course we did. I bought a brown leather overcoat that fit me perfectly, even though it made me look like a Gestapo officer. I couldn't wait for the weather in New York to turn cold so that I could wear my new Nazi coat.

One Saturday night in October, it got really cold, and I finally had the opportunity to wear my new leather coat. I put it on and could not believe that it had shrunk! I did not think that I had gained thirty pounds in a few months because now I couldn't button it. Anyhow, I wore it and we went out to dinner at Quo Vadis, a very chic restaurant in Manhattan. After dinner, in the lobby, we met some old friends, Al and Sue. Al was upset because he hadn't brought a coat with him, and it was freezing outside.

He admired my leather coat which was unbuttoned, only because I couldn't button it.

I explained the story of the coat and jokingly, I asked him if he would like to buy it from me.

He jumped at the opportunity, we worked a deal, and he left wearing my beautiful shrunken leather coat.

I went home cold, wondering whether the coat would shrink some more, and whether Al would have to resell it to a midget!

NIXON AND THE SAUNA

THE BIG NEWS story emanating from Washington in 1973 and 1974 was all about President Nixon and Watergate. The president had made some audiotapes that were missing, and if they were found, they could lead to his downfall. The "not fake news" newspapers and television programs were having a party with these stories.

At this time, there was a gasoline shortage and it became a great difficulty to have one's car filled with gas. Kathy and I became friendly with Carmine, who owned the Texaco gas station in Fort Lee, and he gave us priority on the gas line. He truly was a lifesaver.

One Sunday morning, in the sauna at the local gym, Carmine was holding court with his boys. I walked in and heard an unbelievable conversation. Sweating profusely, Carmine said, "My wife's cousin has a friend who is married to a woman who works in Washington DC and listened to the tapes. She says that President Nixon said on the tapes — blah blah blah blah!"

The FBI, the CIA, and other government agencies were all searching for the tapes. But only Carmine's wife's cousin's friend's wife had heard the tapes. Carmine's friends in the sauna, all looking to fill up their gas tanks, told Carmine that they were sure that his story was true.

Sadly enough, so did I!

DADDY'S HOME!

M Y TWO FAVORITE words were "Daddy's home!"
I have always said that you get out of your children just what you put in. I was always there for my kids, and now they are always there for me. Being the father to three girls was hard work, but the rewards were absolutely well worth it.

Every evening, when one of them spotted me in the driveway and screamed, "Daddy's home," no matter how bad my day had been, everything was now terrific!

Jennifer, age six, and Heather, age three, starred in a Ronzoni television commercial. Kathy's cousin's boyfriend worked for an advertising agency and needed two beautiful kids to eat spaghetti for a commercial. They looked terrific, the commercial was a success, but there was no budget and they were not paid. My mother was living in West Palm Beach, and she loved seeing the girls on television. She called the local stations and got a schedule of when that particular commercial was being shown, and she watched it regularly. She was truly happy and proud seeing her grandchildren as tv stars!

***

I had two tickets for many years to the Giants' games, and each week I took one daughter with me. Of course, they knew nothing about football, but they fought and argued about who would be going that week. They took coloring books and made believe they knew what was going on. They cheered when the Giants scored a touchdown and then would say, "Dad, can we leave now?"

***

Kathy and I went to a wedding without the girls in Montréal in 1976. We had lunch in a great Chinese restaurant and learned that we could take food home with us, that would be packaged with dry ice to keep it cold. We brought the package of food home with us on the plane. When we got home, I told the girls that I had a real surprise for them. I filled the bathtub with water and put the sheets of dry ice into the tub. When the girls saw the bubbles in the tub, they freaked out, and forty years later, they still talk about it!

On a cold February weekend in 1979, Kathy and I went to the Ocean Club in the Bahamas, and Kathy's mother watched the children. We had a suite with a private pool and realized that this setup would be great for the kids. We made lengthy arrangements for the girls to fly down by themselves and so eleven-year-old Jennifer, eight-year-old Heather, and five-year-old Vanessa flew by themselves to the Bahamas. We all had the best weekend.

Just after we moved to Great Neck in 1980, my girls reported a squeaking sound coming from the basement. Convinced that it was a mouse, I called a local exterminator. He set traps all around the basement, but no mouse was caught and I still heard the squeak. Then, he set more traps and the basement looked like a minefield. Determined to track down the mouse, I sat in the basement for a while reading my newspaper. Finally, I heard the squeak, but it was coming from the ceiling. Very embarrassed, I realized that the squeak was coming from the smoke detector.

Mickey Mouse had fooled me!

***

My three girls were interested in seeing my old neighborhood, so one Sunday we drove from Great Neck to Brighton Beach. I showed them the building that I lived in on Brighton 12th Street, and across the street, my school, P.S. 225, and of course the schoolyard where I played ball. They saw the movie theater, the Oceana, and Norm and Phil's luncheonette, where I worked as a youth. I bought hot dogs for the family at Zei Mar, the great Brighton deli.

I showed them Brighton Beach Baths, where I had spent so many summers. Even though it was winter, the club was open that day, and we went to the front desk. The guard at the desk was giving me a hard time about entering, but I worked it out with him. Jennifer asked me, "Why was that old man so mean to you. He was really old."

I didn't tell her that I recognized him from the neighborhood, and that old man was a freshman when I was a senior. That day, I felt ancient!

***

Cooking is not my specialty. But what I liked to make was spaghetti with my special sauce. The sauce was butter and ketchup! My kids loved this dish and always asked me to make it for them. I told them that I had a secret recipe that I would tell no one about. One night, I was preparing it and as a joke, next to the butter and ketchup, I purposely left out a can of Ajax and dishwasher detergent. When the girls saw this, they freaked out! Of course, I told them this was all a joke and they laughed.

***

In 1982 I was given four tickets to a Mets game, and my girls were all excited to go. I loved baseball and a Mets game was always on our television, but my kids had no interest watching. As we were driving to Shea Stadium, we played a game: I would give them the name of the city and they would give me the name of the team. These were some of the answers:

Boston - Cream Pie
Philadelphia - Cream Cheese
Philadelphia - Cheesesteak
New York - Sirloin
I guess they were hungry!

***

One Sunday I had an idea that I knew they would love. I told them that we would drive somewhere, but they would have to be blindfolded as this was a surprise. They all agreed and I drove them to Manhattan to the heliport. They took off their blindfolds and were delighted to know that they were going on a helicopter ride over the city. They loved it!

When I was a boy, my father often took me to the Automat, and

I loved to eat the baked macaroni. There was only one Automat left in the city (on East 42nd Street) and Kathy and I went to a surprise party there one Saturday night. I figured that my girls would love the concept and the food, so I drove them there the next night for dinner. I told them that the macaroni was the best, and I bought four orders, and needless to say, they hated it. Guess who ate four orders of baked macaroni casserole?

***

Around 1985, I got tickets to see *Porgy and Bess* at Radio City Music Hall. Everyone loved the show, especially me, and after the show ended, we headed home down East 49th Street. Stuck in traffic, I noticed two men fighting on the ground to the left of me. One man was testing to see how hard the sidewalk was by banging the other man's head on the sidewalk.

I shouted for them to stop fighting, and when they did not, I stupidly got out of the car to try to break up the fight. When they saw me, they stopped fighting, and when I realized that the man on top had a gun in his back pocket, I jumped back in my car. My kids were screaming and the men were still fighting. But at least, I did my good deed for the day!

***

Over Christmas vacation that year, we took a family trip to London and Paris. The highlight of the trip was when we first got to London at 7 a.m., our rooms were not ready. I convinced the manager, for twenty pounds, that we must have at least one room now. He gave us one small room with one small bed, and the five Karps slept soundly for a few hours in that very narrow bed at the famous Brown's Hotel!

***

Many years later, when Rita passed away in 2013, my three girls immediately flew to Florida to be with their Dad. I wrote a wonderful eulogy that I wanted to read at the funeral, but I didn't know whether I could make it all the way through without breaking up. My three beautiful daughters stood behind me for support and knowing that they were there, I made it through.

Daddy's home!

Top - Mustached George driving Jennifer and Heather in 1973 —
Host Farm in Pennsylvania.
Bottom - My three beauties in Florida in 1975.

Vanessa, Heather, and Jennifer are flower girls at
Danny's wedding in 1976.
A favorite picture!

GEORGE, THE HANDYMAN

I N THE WINTER of 1974, the Karps had just moved into our new house in Oradell, New Jersey. This was the first house I had ever owned and I was so proud and so thrilled to live there. We had a big unfinished basement, and one of the first things I did in my new house was to buy a set of electric trains for all of us (especially me) to play with in the basement.

My back was hurting and I realized that my mattress was too soft, and therefore I needed a wooden bed board to place under the mattress. I measured the bed and headed to the neighborhood lumberyard with my six-year-old daughter, Jennifer. When I gave the lumberman the dimensions of the bed, he looked at me strangely and said that this bed must have been built for Kareem Abdul-Jabbar, a seven foot basketball player. Indignantly, I said, "Do you think that I am an idiot and don't know how to use a tape measure?"

He was right, I must be an idiot!

He cut the board to my dimensions, and with difficulty I lifted it to the roof of my car. I had rope and tied it to the roof with me holding the left side and Jennifer struggling to hold the right side. The ride home was precarious!

I carried the board upstairs with difficulty and placed it on my bed. The man was right — the board *was* built for Kareem Abdul-Jabbar!

Now I had a choice. I could carry the board downstairs, tie it again to the roof of my car, bring it back to the man, admit that I was an idiot, and buy a smaller board that I would again tie to the roof of my car and carry upstairs.

Or, keep the board and with an electric saw (which I did not own, naturally) cut the board to my dimensions. The latter choice seemed easier, so I went out and bought an electric saw, most certainly not from the lumberyard. Unfortunately, the board was made of plywood and was almost impossible to cut through. It took forever but I accomplished it, very slowly. However, there was a mountain of sawdust all around the room. It was about ten degrees outside and I had to open all the windows in the room to try to get the sawdust out. Besides that, my back was aching!

My wife Kathy, who was not home, returned, and saw this fiasco. She sarcastically said, "If ever your business gets bad, you can always become a handyman!"

Very funny!

HOUSE BEAUTIFUL

ANOTHER INTERESTING STORY took place a few weeks after we moved into our new home in Oradell. Coming from a small apartment in Fort Lee to a large house meant that the new house had to be furnished, of course using a fancy decorator of Kathy's choosing. We were not quite ready for House Beautiful — buying a new washing machine or a new garden hose was more on the agenda.

Heather, my middle daughter, had met a little girl on the next block and her father, Bobby, was coming to pick her up. He had just moved into his big house and was in the same situation as us. He looked at my big empty house and cleverly said, "We must be using the same decorator!"

That was a great line that I remember after forty years.

ONCE IN LOVE WITH HARRY

MY MOM AND her second husband Harry came to visit us in New Jersey in the spring of 1975. I picked them up at the airport and waited for their luggage. Instead of one big suitcase, they brought with them about ten little plaid suitcases. Mom said that they were easier to carry; maybe she was right (if she had ten hands).

On Saturday, I was washing my car in the driveway, when a bug flew into my ear. As much as I tried, I couldn't get it out, but then I had an idea. I put the hose next to my ear and tried to flush the bug out. This had to be a strange sight for Harry, who had just come out of the house.

In disbelief, he asked me what I was doing, seeing the hose in my hand next to my ear. I told him that I was on the phone. I think that he believed me!

Even though it was now June, we had a cool morning. I didn't want to turn on the heat, because I knew that the house would warm up quickly during the day. Harry was cold and he came down to breakfast wearing his hat and earmuffs. My girls had a good laugh at this sight.

Knowing that there was no gourmet dining in Century Village in West Palm Beach, I took Mom and Harry to an expensive French restaurant, near our house in Oradell. We all had great meals and on the way home, I asked Harry if he had enjoyed his meal, which he had devoured.

"It was all right," he said, "but can we stop at a diner for coffee and cake?"

"Maybe tomorrow," I replied, holding back a burp!

MY FIRST MERCEDES

I HAD TO TAKE a business trip to Los Angeles in 1976 and I needed to rent a car for a few days. A friend of mine told me of a car rental company that rented luxury cars and I was excited. I was able to rent a new Mercedes convertible, a 450 SL. I fell in love with this car.

When I came home, I only had one thing on my mind and that was, I had to have that car. I got my wish and on election day 1976, Jimmy Carter was elected president, but more importantly, I got a new Mercedes, a silver 450 SL convertible!

I was told that I should not wash or wax the car for a few weeks so I waited and waited. Finally on Thanksgiving day, I got my chance, and in my driveway, I washed and waxed my pride and joy. The new car looked so good that I could not resist; so on the next day, Friday, I washed and waxed it again.

There was so much wax on my new car now, that I did not think that I would be able to fit it in my garage!

THE RIGHT DECISION

A CERTAIN DAY IN July 1977 was doubly important to me. I had an appointment at Petrie Stores to discuss a new item from my company, that conceivably could result in a major order for us. I was there at 9 a.m. waiting for the buyer and the merchandise staff. There were salesmen ahead of me, who had appointments at 8 a.m., and everyone was waiting impatiently.

But, today was Parents Visiting Day at Heather's Day Camp, and for my seven-year-old daughter, this was really important. 10 a.m became 11 a.m. which became 12 noon and I was still waiting. Like the song said, should I stay or should I go?

I explained my dilemma to a fellow salesman, an older gentleman, who gave me some good advice. He wisely said, "It's more important to you and especially to your daughter, for you to be with her at Camp. Petrie Day can be tomorrow, but only today is visiting day for your child."

He was right. I left and drove to camp and my daughter was ecstatic! I know I made the right decision.

NO BLOOMINGDALES IN MEXICO

P UERTO VALLARTA IN Mexico was becoming the new hotspot for American tourists. Kathy and I had been to Acapulco many times, and now in 1978, we wanted to make a change. The trip got off to a great start when the airline lost *my* suitcase, not Kathy's. I had a choice to make — I could wear Kathy's underwear and bathing suit, or I could go to town and buy new clothing. Kathy's underwear was too tight, so I went to town looking for Bloomingdale's, but had to settle for Pedro's. Sitting in the sun and getting a tan was ultra-important to me. My rich dermatologist can now attest to that!

The first day we went to the beach, but it was a cloudy day with no sun. The second day was exactly the same as the first day, and I was getting really annoyed with Puerto Vallarta. That evening, we met some friends for dinner, who were staying not at the beach like us, but at a hotel in the mountains. Our friends were all suntanned and we were pale. They said that at their hotel, there was not a cloud in the sky all day, and they invited us to come to their hotel the next day.

They were right. There were no clouds and we loved spending the day and the next day and the next day and the next day, etc.

PS — I'm still waiting for my suitcase!

A LIFE LESSON

MY BUSINESS WAS good in 1977, and Kathy, the girls, and I celebrated the Christmas vacation by going to the very famous, The Breakers Hotel in Palm Beach. My mother lived a short distance away in West Palm Beach, so she was very excited because each night one of the girls would stay with her. Our room at The Breakers was small, but after a consultation with the manager, and a timely Chanukah present for him, our tiny room became a gigantic room!

I rented a white Chevy convertible for the week, and I hoped that it would not rain. The first night, I requested my car, but I noticed something unusual. My full gas tank was now half full and there were cigarette butts in the ashtray. I figured that the parking attendant might have been smoking, but I did not understand the gas situation.

The second day was even more unusual. There were no cigarette butts in the ashtray and the gas tank was full. I investigated and found that there was another Mr. Karp registered at the hotel, who also was driving a white Chevy convertible! After that when I had to request my car, I gave my room number.

The weather was beautiful for the week, my kids had a great time, my mother was happy, and I started to love being in Florida — an omen for the future!

The night before we were leaving, I thought it would be a good idea to pay my bill early, thus avoiding the big crush in the morning. I was told that I couldn't pay before morning, but I could look at my bill now.

I don't remember exactly how much it was, but let's say hypothetically, for my ten days, it was three thousand dollars (remember, this was 1977).

We were all packed, and the next morning I went down to pay my bill, and there was a mob scene in the lobby. The cashier told me that I owed only two hundred dollars, and I told her that I thought she was wrong, in fact, I owed much more. She double checked and said two hundred dollars was the correct figure. I asked her to get the manager to review my bill, and Mr. Manager told me to pay the two hundred dollars and hit the road. I wrote a check for that amount and had the bill stamped "paid in full."

I deduced that the other Mr. Karp had paid my bill in error, and I wondered how long it would take Mr. Karp and The Breakers to figure this one out. Well, it took seven months and after a few letters and phone calls, I was now faced with a decision. I could write a check to The Breakers for twenty-eight hundred dollars or do nothing at all.   I sat down with my three kids and tried to simply explain the situation. I told them that even though I did not have to pay the hotel, I was going to pay. They realized that I would be cheating the hotel by not paying them. Paying the bill was the right and honorable thing to do.

Ten-year-old Jennifer, seven-year-old Heather, and four-year-old Vanessa all learned an important life lesson!

Now forty years later, thanks to The Breakers, none of my children have ever landed in jail!

THE GARBAGE MAN

THERE WAS A sudden citywide power outage in July 1977 that devastated New York City. That night, all over the city, looting and rioting took place in a disgraceful and violent manner.

The morning news reported the situation and said that power should be restored very soon. I had an important appointment in my office that morning, and I was anxious to get to work. But since my office was on the 16th floor, I didn't want to climb sixteen flights to be alone in an unairconditioned office. So I waited.

I got dressed to go to work, awaiting the word that power had been restored in the city. I was wearing my new navy blue suit with a colorful tie and I looked pretty darn dapper! I was outside and noticed that the garbageman was down the street picking up garbage. I realized that I was living in my house for three years, but I had never met the garbage man. I went down to the curb to speak to the man and told him, "If you worked in New York City, you would have the day off today."

The man was huge, weighing three hundred pounds, and he was sweating profusely. Flies were buzzing around his head. He eyed me up and down, looking at my new suit and asked,

"Man, are you in f——g sanitation?"

A question like that does not deserve an answer!

MY ACHING BACK

IN THE 70s and 80s, my Achilles' heel, the weak spot of my body, was not my heel but rather my back.

Vacationing at La Costa, the fabulous spa in Southern California, I was playing tennis one morning, and as I lunged for a low ball at the net, I threw out my back. Not being able to continue, I hobbled to the spa. I figured that if I had an injury, there would be no better place to be injured, than at La Costa. Dr. Smith, the longtime physician, was on duty at the spa, and I told him that I was hurting. "Would I be better off icing my back or rather using heat?", I asked, in pain.

"Young man, that's a great question," he replied, scratching his bald head. "Try heat."

I decided to follow his instructions, and went to the spa, sat in the boiling whirlpool, and used all the hot gadgets available. The next morning, I could barely get out of bed. I was twisted like a pretzel. I went to see Dr. Smith again in my twisted condition, and he scratched his bald head again and muttered, "I guess I should have said ice."

I'm sure that he graduated last at medical school, if in fact he went to medical school!

***

A few years later, in 1982, my back was hurting and I went to see a local chiropractor.

My nine-year-old daughter, Vanessa, accompanied me to the doctor, whom I called "Captain Crunch." He was manipulating me, and I guess

I was making unpleasant noises, so my daughter peeked into the room. When she saw what Captain Crunch was doing to her papa, she started to cry.

I never went back to that chiropractor again and Vanessa gave up eating Captain Crunch. Now, she only eats Cheerios!

Five years later, I hurt my back playing tennis, as usual. I was really in bad shape with back pain and sciatic leg pain, but I was able to get an appointment with Dr. John Sarno, the renowned back specialist. He told me that my pain was emotionally induced, but in six weeks, I would be fine. We had a reservation at Canyon Ranch in Tucson in a few weeks, and I really wanted to go. So I went. As I descended slowly from the plane, I told Kathy that I wanted to play tennis that week. She laughed at me and said, "How can you play tennis? You can barely walk."

I endured the pain, made an appointment with the tennis pro for later in the week, and actually got out on the court and hit with the pro for thirty minutes. I felt great and knew that my bad days were behind me. Two weeks later, I played in my regular tennis game at home.

I read and reread the book that Dr. Sarno had given me, and after fifty readings, I guess I finally understood what he was talking about. Thank goodness my back has not really bothered me for a long, long time.

Dr. Sarno, thank you, wherever you are!

ROAD RAGE

IT WAS A cold Saturday night in February 1977. Kathy and I were on our way to a dinner party that our friends Carol and Stanley were giving in their apartment in Fort Lee. I was driving south on Forest Avenue from our home in Oradell. My car was in the left lane of this two-lane road, and maybe I was driving a trifle slow. Right behind me was a car, growing impatient with my slow driving, so he flashed his bright lights in my rearview mirror. I became annoyed and moved to the right lane so he could pass me on my left side. Still bothered, I moved to the left lane, right behind him. Now it was my turn to flash my bright lights into his rearview mirror.

Road rage is boiling!

He moved to the right lane, rolled down his window, and started screaming at me. I screamed at him, but my windows were rolled up. Kathy was loving this altercation. Finally, he motioned to roll down my window so I could hear him. I complied and he screamed at me, **"Let's fight!"**

I yelled back at him, "You got it, pal. Let's do it."

He screamed, "Make the first right turn!"

I responded, "Absolutely!".

He immediately made a right turn into the first street off the road, awaiting me. I stepped on the gas, going about eighty miles an hour, straight ahead to Route 4. Kathy looked at me strangely.

"I'm disappointed," she said. "Why didn't you fight him?"

"I just took a shower and don't want to mess up my hair! Besides, I'm a lover not a fighter."

Soon after, I was in Fort Lee enjoying a fine meal. This moron was still standing in the snow, waiting for me, polishing his brass knuckles!

NEXT YEAR IN JERUSALEM

O NE OF THE most important days in the history of Israel took place in November 1977. The president of Egypt, Anwar el-Sadat, traveled to Jerusalem, for the first time, to meet Israeli Prime Minister Menachem Begin. And most important, I was there in Jerusalem to witness this historic meeting. Actually, I didn't witness the meeting personally, but I was in Jerusalem at that time.

This was my first trip to Israel; I have since been back three more times. Kathy and I went with a UJA group from Bergen County, New Jersey, to visit the Jewish homeland. We saw Jerusalem, Tel Aviv, the Dead Sea, and we climbed Masada. I didn't actually climb Masada, I took the elevator! We met many interesting people on the trip and became friendly with several.

One new friend Dan was a knowledgeable baseball fan, and he knew that I was a master of baseball trivia. He asked me all kinds of ridiculous questions. "Who played third base for the White Sox in 1911 or who was the substitute catcher for the Cardinals in 1923?"

As much as I knew about baseball, I could not answer these weird questions. But one day, I got him! We were touring a small city in northern Israel, called Safed (pronounced Sfot), and listening to a boring lecture. I approached Dan and asked him a great question, "What famous American baseball player came from this town?"

I had him stumped. I told him the answer, "Babe Ruth was the Sultan of Sfot (the Sultan of SWAT)!"

He laughed for the rest of the trip.

The cost of the trip was minimal because everyone was supposed to make a charitable donation to UJA. But no one approached us about the contribution. Day after day went by and there was no talk about the donation. The last day that we were in Israel, we were taken to Yad Vashem, which was the Israeli memorial to the victims of the Holocaust. This was a very moving and emotional experience and Kathy and I were truly shaken. Leaving the museum, the leader of the trip came over to me, put his arm around me, and asked how much was I going to give to UJA.

I called this "the Yad Vashem hug!"

***

The trip home from Tel Aviv to New York was unbelievably long and it seemed never ending. Complaining to Kathy, I remarked, "When they established the State of Israel, why couldn't they establish it in the State of Pennsylvania!"

PRIDE OF THE YANKEES

HAVING BOUGHT A condo in Westhampton in 1978, I found the commute each summer Sunday night back to New Jersey was truly intolerable. Kathy and the three girls would be sound asleep in the car, and I would be creeping along, listening to them snore. I would be stuck in very heavy traffic, the trip sometimes taking as much as four hours. I loved Westhampton but I hated the commute.

That winter, we toyed with the idea of selling the house in Oradell and perhaps buying a house closer to Westhampton, in Long Island, preferably Great Neck. Then, I had an epiphany!

Free agency in baseball was now becoming widespread. The Yankees had just signed Tommy John, a great pitcher who had a terrific year for the Dodgers. His contract of $575,000 each year for three years was then the biggest free-agent signing in baseball history. Today, the Yankee batboy makes more money than that!

Since I had a terrific house, I figured that Tommy John could well afford the inflated price that I would ask for it. Now how do I get Tommy John to see my house?

My idea — I wrote a letter to Al Rosen, the president of the New York Yankees. I told him all about my house, enclosed some pictures, and suggested that this house would be perfect for his newest employee. I told many people about my letter, and they all thought this was a unique approach.

About two weeks later, just before Christmas, I got a phone call late at night. The voice said, "Hi, Mr. Karp, this is Tommy John of the New

York Yankees. Al Rosen told me about your letter to him and I would be very interested in seeing your house."

Figuring this was one of my friends, I was waiting for laughter but none came.

"Who is this?" I asked.

Again the voice assured me that this was Tommy John. I couldn't believe it! He told me that he would be in New Jersey tomorrow and would like to see the house. We made a date for 2 o'clock the next afternoon, and I made sure that the house was spotless. My kids came home from school early and told their friends that *Elton John* was coming to visit. Of course, they had never heard of Tommy John!

They were doing cartwheels on the front lawn when an old beat up Chevy came rumbling down the block. Tommy John emerged wearing a huge Los Angeles Dodger championship ring that must've weighed five pounds. He was very friendly, took pictures, and said he would tell his pregnant wife all about the house. Since we were contemporaries, I suggested that we all have dinner in the city sometime in the future. I'm still waiting!

A few weeks later, I got a letter from the Yankees saying that Tommy John would not be buying my house. Boo hoo!

He ultimately bought a house in Franklin Lakes, very near his teammate, Ron Guidry. He should have bought my house because two years later, his young son Travis fell from an upstairs window in his new house and was seriously injured. The boy was in a coma for a long while but fortunately recovered.

Tommy John pitched successfully for many more years and actually won 288 games during his long career. His name is in the sports pages every day because of what is known as "Tommy John Surgery," an operation that afflicts so many pitchers today. Since he was the first person to undergo this surgical procedure, his name is attached to it.

Can you imagine if Irving Goldstein was the first person to have this surgery!

SQUARE EGGS

FOR OUR PASSOVER Seder in 1979, I had a special surprise for everyone. Would you believe "square eggs?"

Months earlier in Bloomingdale's, I spotted and bought a novelty item that was Lucite and created square hard-boiled eggs. I realized that this would be a great novelty for Passover and my kids would love it. The night before the Seder, I boiled a dozen eggs, peeled them, put them into the lucite squares, and then put them in the refrigerator. The next evening at sundown, the Seder began and when the time came, I brought out the square eggs. No one could believe they were seeing square hard-boiled aggs. Everyone asked the question, "How could a chicken lay square eggs?"

I answered, "This was from a special chicken who lived near *Times Square!*"

Almost every day, I had lunch at a dairy restuarant, R.Gross, that was probably the best dairy restaurant in Manhattan. One of their specialties was gefilte fish. With Passover coming and knowing that we were having a Seder at our house, I decided to buy and bring home gefilte fish because I knew that everyone would just love this specialty. I bought ten large pieces at ten dollars a piece, quite a hefty price, but I knew it was well worth it. At the Seder with the square eggs, my fancy gefilte fish was served and everyone turned up their noses and said that they didn't like "filtered fish."

Every night for the next week, I stuffed myself with this delicious gefilte fish and square eggs!   Burp!

GETTING EVEN

E VEN THOUGH IT looks easy, real estate business is tricky. I learned this fact the hard way.

We wanted to move from Oradell, New Jersey, to Great Neck, on the north shore of Long Island. Great Neck, in particular, Kings Point, had become a very desirable area for the purchase of a house. The reason for this was that the Shah of Iran was being driven out of his country by the Iranian Fundamentalists. The Shah had many close business associates who were also being forced to leave Iran. In 1979, these wealthy Jewish businessmen chose to come to two areas in the United States — Beverly Hills and Kings Point.

Houses in Kings Point were now very much in demand and the Persians (Iranian had become a dirty word) were scooping up houses at their now inflated prices. Unfortunately for me, trying to buy a house in Kings Point put me in competition with the Persians, and I was losing. We saw many houses and these houses would stay on the market only for a very short time before they were sold to the Persians. Finally, we saw a terrific house and I knew that I could not procrastinate, so we bought it.

I told my friend Stanley that I had bought a house in Great Neck. Knowing that there were nine towns in Great Neck, he asked me in which town had I bought. When I told him that it was Kings Point, he accused me of "reverse snobbery." That was funny!

A wise man once told me, "Never buy a new house before you sell your old house." I did not listen because I thought that since it was so easy to sell a house in Kings Point, it would be just as easy to sell a house in Oradell. WRONG!

We called in the top real estate broker in New Jersey to sell our home, which really was a great house. He loved the house and said that there would be no problem in selling our home. After a year and with many price reductions, I realized that he was wrong, and I decided to try to sell the house myself.

I put an ad in *The New York Times* and got one response, but it was the right response! A man, Mr. P. , was interested in the house even though he knew nothing about New Jersey. He told me that he had a friend in Newark, **only** an hour away. We made an appointment to meet on Saturday at 2 p.m. He and his family came, and they immediately fell in love with the house.

Coincidentally, a broker was coming at 2:30 p.m. with a client to view the house. The P. family was now in the basement, loving the house.

I had an idea, and took a shot and it worked! I told Mr. P. that a young couple were coming at 2:30 p.m. with their parents to buy the house. I fibbed that the young couple had seen the house several times, they loved it, and were ready to buy!

The doorbell rang and I told Mr. P. that the young couple were going to give me a deposit on the house. Mr. P. emphatically said, "No, do not take it, I want to buy your house."

I said, "Okay, will you give me $xxx for the house? If you do, I will send them away and tell them the house is sold to another party."

He shook my hand and unbelievably told me, "Yes, we have a deal."

The broker was showing the house to a woman who did not even like the house. In a very loud voice that could be heard from the basement, I said, "I'm sorry, but the house has been sold."

The broker and the woman looked at me in disbelief.

Mr. P. and his family were delighted, I opened a bottle of champagne, and in two days a contract was signed. The hard-to-sell house was finally sold!

A few months later, at the closing for the house, Mr. P. aggravated me over a very minor matter, and I was forced to give him a large rebate.

I was really angry with him because he was not being fair with me. But I vowed to get even with him.

We had remained friendly with Mal and Elaine, who lived just across the street from our house. Mal told me that Mr. P. was a pain in the butt, and all of the neighbors disliked him. He had a German Shepherd that he kept outside at night and this big dog barked incessantly, keeping everyone up. Mr. P. refused to bring the dog inside and the whole neighborhood was fuming.

I told Mal that I had a way he could get even with Mr. P. At our closing, I had given Mr. P. only one garage door opener because I could not find the second one. But, the second one had turned up and now I gave it to Mal. Now, every night, Mal would get up at 2 a.m., use the clicker and open Mr. P.'s garage door. Every night, lights would go on in Mr. P's house and Mr. P. would be scurrying around the garage.

I think Mr. P. thought that the house was haunted!

BEATEN BY A TEN YEAR OLD

COULD FEDERER OR Djokovic or Nadal be beaten by a ten-year-old kid? Impossible!

We were just settling into our new condo in Westhampton in 1979 and we invited some friends for lunch and the beach, one Sunday afternoon. Andrew was a precocious ten-year-old who was taking tennis lessons. His mother was convinced that her little boy was the next John McEnroe, and announced that Andrew would love to play tennis with me.

Reluctantly, I agreed and after hitting a few balls, Andrew asked me if we could play a game. Since I was hungry for a victory, I said sure and we started to play. Andrew was running me all over the court, and he was beating the hell out of me. Finally, he beat me 6 - 3.

We went back to the beach, where he loudly announced to the world, "I just beat George Karp 6-3!"

Andrew's mother said to me, "George, you are the best sport, letting my little Andrew beat you." I certainly did not tell her that I busted my butt trying to keep up with this little upstart!

That's me, practicing a volley at the beach in Westhampton - 1980.

PAIN PILLS

I RAN INTO AN old classmate Ronnie, one day in Westhampton in 1979. He was thinking of buying a condo at the Yardarm, where we were living. I showed him our apartment, he loved it, and he decided to buy a unit for himself.

That morning at tennis, I had hurt my back, for a change. My friend Ronnie had become a doctor and when I told him about my back, he quickly wrote out a prescription for me to ease my back pain. I told him that it wasn't serious, but he insisted that I fill the prescription and take the pills. I followed doctor's orders and took the pills. What a mistake!

The next morning, I could barely move and I was in terrible pain. My good friend Dr. Ronnie, instead of giving me pain relieving pills, had given me pain pills!

A few years later, my pain gone, Ronnie invited us to a party at his apartment. He told me that a few old Lincoln High School friends would be there, and that I would have a good time.

I recognized everyone there and was happy to see each person, except for one old nemesis. John was a year ahead of me in school and he was the sports editor of the *Lincoln Log*, the school newspaper. As a junior, I was the associate sports editor and really wanted to be the sports editor in my senior year. John's duty was to select the next year's sports editor from the rest of the juniors on the staff.

I was really disappointed when he selected Larry to be the sports editor in our senior year. Rumor had it that Larry, who lived near John, used to carry John's books home from school.

At the party, I confronted John and he vehemently denied the story. He told me that I could verify that with Larry, who was now John's chauffeur and was waiting for John downstairs in the parking lot!

A MERRY CHRISTMAS IN HAITI

EVERY CHRISTMAS VACATION in the 1970s, the Karp family traveled to West Palm Beach to see my mother. Nanny had passed away in April 1980, so there was no need to go to Florida. Instead, Kathy and I decided to take the girls on a different vacation — a Club Med vacation.

Being a joker, I had a great idea that the kids would ultimately love. I told them that their mother and I were going on vacation, but without them. A babysitter would be in charge, and they were not too happy. *Of course,* the girls would be going with us, but it would be a grand surprise. A brand-new Club Med in Haiti had just opened, and I made a reservation for five people.

Kathy secretly packed their summer stuff for them and hid the suitcases. The day of departure came and I said to them, "Would you like to go to the airport with us, to see us off? Our taxi will wait and take you home."

The children all wanted to go to the airport and when we got there, again I asked, "Would you like to go on the plane until it's ready to take off. The stewardess will make an announcement and then you can leave."

They thought this would be adventurous, so we all got on the plane. The doors closed, the plane started to move, and the girls started to scream.

"Surprise, we are all going to Club Med in Haiti," I announced.

The kids seemed very surprised, but I had a sneaking suspicion that all along they knew that they were going!

After we landed, we drove through Haiti until we got to the hotel. All of us could not believe the living conditions of the Haitian people; it was a far cry from anything that any of us had ever seen, anywhere in the United States. We arrived at the hotel and were shown our rooms. The walls of the rooms were made of cinderblock, and I think they filmed the movie, *Papillon*, in my room, when Steve McQueen was held in solitary confinement!

There was a nude beach at Club Med, which my kids soon discovered. They laughed and laughed and laughed!

I got involved in a coed volleyball game, men against the women. There were many French people at the resort, and to say the least, they were uninhibited. One beautiful French woman, across the net from me, was playing topless. Also, this very busty mademoiselle had painted her body, and it looked unbelievable. I could not keep my eye on the ball; I only could keep my eye on the woman! The men lost the game, 21-0.

Jennifer got stung by a jellyfish, Heather won a prize, and Vanessa loved the nude beach. The highlight, or the lowlight, of the vacation was when Kathy and I took a walk on the nude beach one afternoon. She dared me to take off my bathing suit and go in the water. I took her dare, disrobed, and asked her to watch my Speedo as I ran into the water.

She also ran — ran away with my bathing suit.

What to do? I could stay in the water until dark, but I was afraid of sharks. I could run naked, across the grounds to my room but that would be too embarrassing. Fortunately, my wife who thought this was hilarious finally came back with my bathing suit.

The next day, I debated seeing a Haitian divorce lawyer!

BACK IN THE U.S.S.R

SOMETIMES I SAY things and people don't have the slightest idea what I'm talking about. I had a designer Neville, working for me in 1980, at the time that John Lennon of the Beatles was murdered. We met for an appointment and I could see that Neville was really out of it. I asked her if she was okay, and she started to cry and said, "I'm so upset that Lennon was killed."

Sympathetically, I said, "I understand just how you feel. I felt badly when Stalin died."

She looked at me blankly, not knowing what the hell I was talking about!

HIGH SOCIETY

W E WERE NOT part of Westhampton's so-called "society," but friends of ours were, and we were invited to a fancy society party in 1980. The party was held in a very big house on Dune Road — not too shabby! The owner of the house, Norman, was an executive in the publishing industry, and there were plenty of Waspy people in attendance.

The highlight of the evening was a line spoken by the executive. A group of us were talking to Norman and a lady boldly asked him a question. "Norman, I must know… are you Jewish?"

Waspy Norman glared at the lady and finally said, "Madam, two of my best friends are Jewish — my mother and my father!"

I loved his response and have been waiting all these years for someone to ask me that question, so that I can use Norman's classic line.

MADAM BUTTERFLY

THE SUMMER OF 1981 was winding down. My children were back from summer camp, and Kathy and I had returned from a trip to Europe. Heather, eleven years old, and I decided to take a leisurely walk on the beach in Westhampton. There had been rumors that women were going topless at the seashore, but certainly not at *our* Yardarm beach.

We walked for a while and approached the Bath & Tennis Club of Westhampton. Someone called to me and waved to me to come over. As we approached, I recognized a lady that I did business with. She was the sportswear buyer for Alexander's (now an organization of blessed memory). I viewed her as being a very conservative and straight businesswoman.

But now, I viewed her as topless! Heather was embarrassed but not as embarrassed as me.

I didn't know where to look — her toes, my toes, or Heather's toes. We talked for a while, then Heather and I left and we both jumped in the ocean to cool off.

Back in the city, I continued to do business with her but never mentioned her boobs or her toes!

***

About a year later, something even weirder happened. I was attempting to do business with a young female buyer from a California chain of stores, in her office. I was showing her a new group of printed

T-shirts, the best one being a colorful butterfly. She quietly said to me, " Do you want to see a really beautiful butterfly?"

"Sure," I answered, not knowing what to expect.

"Then close the door, turn around, and shut your eyes," the young lady said.

I did what she requested and then I heard a zipper sound. I turned around and saw a beautiful butterfly on her shapely tush! I just could not believe it!

The bottom line was that fortunately I saw her butterfly, but unfortunately she did not buy my butterfly.

BOCA BEACH BARGAIN

I
s it possible to love something and to hate it, both at the same time? In this case, yes!

Visiting south Florida for Thanksgiving 1981, we encountered rainy weather. Kathy and I took a ride touring Boca Raton and saw a new country club complex called Boca West. Some Great Neck neighbors were living there and were raving about it. We entered the complex, looked around and loved it. A sales agent showed us a few apartments, and he made the easiest and fastest deal imaginable. Normally, I would think over a situation practically, but in this case, I shot from the hip and quickly bought an apartment!

Kathy bought furniture for the apartment, and when the family arrived for Christmas, everything was set. My kids had many friends in Boca West, and they loved it. But the best part, or maybe the worst part, was that I was able to buy a membership for the Boca Beach Club for one year for only five hundred dollars! This was the deal of the century, or so I thought.

This was my typical day:

I played tennis every morning from 8 a.m. to 10 a.m. Then I returned to the apartment where everyone was waiting for me so that we could drive to the Boca Beach Club. I would pick up a few of my kids' friends and then drive my packed, rented compact car to the club. I dropped off everyone at the club, but since it was now past 11 o'clock, the garage was always full. I had to drive back across the bridge and park my car on the mainland at the Boca Hotel, but of course, the bridge was usually up and

I had to wait. Then, I had to take the ferry across the inlet to get back to the club, and of course, I usually just missed the ferry.

I would finally get to the club at noon, and I would just want to sit in the sun in my rented cabana. But my kids, happy to see their father, would tell me that they were hungry and want to have lunch. We would go down to the restaurant, and of course, we have to wait and wait for a table. Finally, we would have lunch with Dad paying for about ten people.

Now it's 2 o'clock, and I would just like to sit down and lie in the sun at my cabana. One of my children would invariably say, "Can we go home now because we're bored?"

Not happy, I would go down to the ferry and of course, it had just left. When it returned, I would go across to get my car, and I find that there were about two hundred people waiting to get their cars. When I would finally get my car, I would go to the bridge, that would be in the up position. For sure, family and friends would not be there waiting for me, so I would have to double park and search for everybody. After everyone had been rounded up, we would drive home to Boca West, and of course get stuck in traffic.

Now it's 4 o'clock. I'm exhausted with no sunburn, and everyone is all excited about going back to the Boca Beach Club, tomorrow. I can hardly wait!

At the end of the season, I evaluated my experience in Florida. I *loved* Boca West, mainly because my family loved it, but I just *hated* the whole concept of the Boca Beach Club!

The next year, I got a notice that the five hundred dollar deal was no longer in place. I was just delighted!

MY BEST HAIRCUT

I WAS A REGULAR customer of Aldo, in the Plaza Hotel, who had given me terrific haircuts for about ten years. In 1981, I told him that I was going to Italy for two weeks, and I would be missing my regular appointment with him. But, he told me that he had a friend, a barber in Rome, who could cut my hair. Aldo gave me directions to his shop and when I got to Rome, I decided to find the Roman barber.

Aldo's directions were confusing, and I walked around for a while until I found the barbershop. English was barely spoken, but I think I got the barber to understand just what I was saying. Anyway, the Roman barber Bippo started to work on me and he worked and he worked and he worked. He cut my hair, put on oil, put on cream, washed my hair, put on oil, put on cream, etc. Then he took a candle, lit it, and singed my hair. I thought my head was on fire!

Finally, Bippo was finished. I looked in the mirror and I saw a movie star. I thought I was Warren Beatty in *The Roman Spring of Mrs. Stone*.

I didn't wash my hair for a week!

When I got back to New York, I went to see Aldo and told him that I got a terrific haircut from his friend Bippo. Aldo had no idea who Bippo was, and he told me that I had gone to the wrong barbershop!

Regardless, thanks to Bippo, I got the best haircut of my life!

HERE'S JOHNNY!

THE SUMMER OF 1981 was special.

Business was good, our new house was great, my three kids were in summer camp, and as I said previously, Kathy and I went to Italy. We started our trip in Milan and then took the train to Florence to see *David*. We stayed in a beautiful hotel in Florence, but there was a problem. The hotel overlooked the River Arno, but the main road of Italy was just outside my window and it was unbelievably noisy. It was like sleeping alongside the Long Island Expressway!

Sleepless for two nights, I finally bought a package of cotton, which I stuffed into my ears. I liked the cotton so much that I debated keeping it in my ears for the rest of the trip! We rented a car and drove to Venice where my feet got wet, and then we flew to Rome.

The Roman hotel's workers were on strike, so I had to schlepp our suitcases up five flights of stairs. Lovely! Having breakfast the first morning in Rome with our friends Lenny and Sue, we noticed Johnny Carson sitting across the room.

Our first stop that morning was the Vatican and who did we see admiring the Sistine Chapel — Johnny Carson. We had lunch at a nice outdoor restaurant near the fountain of Trevi, and who is sitting at a nearby table, you guessed it — Johnny Carson.

I got up from our table, went to his table and told him this was the third time this morning that I had seen him. He laughed and said that we were both hanging around the right places!

From Rome we went to Naples and then down the Amalfi Coast

with a taxi driver, who now probably owns Uber! I was reading the green Michelin tour book when the driver said to me, "You're Jewish, aren't you?"

I was surprised by that question and asked him why he asked. He responded, "Only Jewish people read the green book!"

Our last stop was at an elegant hotel on Capri. The next morning after breakfast we went down the tram to explore the town. In the plaza, who was sitting at a table having coffee, but Johnny Carson. We had to pass his table, and he looked up and said, "Hi there, I recognize you from Rome. I'm Johnny Carson and this is my wife Joanna."

I didn't say that I was from Mars and did not own a television set, so we shook hands and I introduced Kathy and myself.

After dinner at the hotel, Kathy and I went to look at the shops in town. Suddenly, someone grabbed my sleeve and whispered, "We've got to stop meeting like this!"

It was my new best friend — Johnny Carson!

GOLDBERG THE SPY

THE LONG PLANE ride home from Italy was interesting. We had two bulkhead seats in the middle section that was four seats across. Sitting next to me was a young Italian woman (#1) with a screaming infant (#2) in her lap. The woman's mama (#3) was sitting a few rows back, next to a little boy (#4), whose mother (#5) was sitting next to the screaming baby (#2).

Not wanting to hear a howling baby for eight hours, I did a careful analysis and made a few switches. Mommy (#1) and baby (#2) were now sitting next to mama (#3) back a few rows, and the little boy (#4) was sitting next to his mother, (#5) next to me. Are you confused?

The American mother (#5) did not stop talking. She told me that she was coming from Saudi Arabia, where her husband (#6) worked for an American airplane company, doing work for the Saudis. She gave me all kinds of information about Saudi Arabia that the CIA would love to have.

A few seats away, a well-dressed man (#7) was reading a newspaper that was written in Hebrew. I started a conversation and this Israeli man was very friendly. I told him about the lady giving information to me, and said that if I were a spy, the information would be invaluable. Immediately, he got up from his seat, went to the men's room and avoided me the rest of the trip.

There is an old joke called "Goldberg the Spy". I think this man was actually Goldberg!

HERE'S JOHNNY, YET AGAIN!

THE SUMMER OF 1982 was going to be the summer in France (l'ete en France).   Even though I studied French in high school and in college, I was more fluid rather than fluent in French. I decided to buy some audiotapes that I could play in my car when I commuted to work to reacquaint myself with the French language. For several weeks, I listened to Monsieur Didier and tried to absorb as much French as I could.

At my sister Arlene's house, I ran into Richie, who was my brother-in-law, Harvey's brother.   I had just gotten a new car, a Mercedes convertible, that I loved. Richie was impressed with the car but did not believe me when I told him that the car was so special that it spoke French. He got into the car with me, I started it and he heard Monsieur Didier babbling in French.

Richie was flabbergasted!

***

Kathy and I went to Paris, loved it, rented a car, and drove south. One night, we stayed in a great old château and decided to eat in a very luxurious restaurant that was highly recommended. The ride to the restaurant at twilight, on a winding road through the mountains, was unbelievably scenic. But there were no lights on the winding road, and I was terrified of having to drive this road in the dark, on our return to the château. We had a great meal and the owner of the restaurant told me about a road that was drivable, but it was far out of the way. I decided to take it even though we would not get back to the hotel until after midnight. Finally, we reached the château only to find the main gate locked.

The only thing for me to do was to climb this high fence in the dark. I had never climbed a fence in my life before, always too afraid to do it, but now, at age 43, this was the time to overcome my fear. And, I did it! All that I could think of was the Peggy Lee song, "Is that all there is." I woke up the manager who came down with a huge dog and opened the gate for me.   Oh, what a night!

***

Finally we arrived at the French Riviera and checked into a lovely hotel, the Hotel du Cap. Our room was hot and small, but Bill Cosby was staying next door, so I figured it couldn't be too bad. The next day, I spoke to Bill Cosby about the baseball All-Star game and other worldly matters (but not women)! I took a picture with him and sent it to my kids at camp, who later told me that they had never heard of Bill Cosby.

That afternoon, sitting in this very fancy restaurant of this very fancy hotel, we ordered a big bowl of vegetables. Then it hit me! I decided that when I finally write my autobiography, the title would be, "From Crude to Crudités!"

Our small hot room was too much to endure, so I spoke to the manager about getting a larger room. Of course there was none until I gave him an early Christmas present in July, and I was escorted to a beautiful junior suite, being told that we had to share a patio with our next-door neighbor.

I went outside and met my next-door neighbor.

Unbelievably, it was my best friend from Italy — Johnny Carson!

He remembered us, was very friendly, and when we left, he asked, "Where do we meet next summer?"

Guess who made the cover of Newsweek?
I still have that sweater!

DON'T JUDGE A BOOK BY ITS COVER

"WHO ARE YOU to judge people without knowing them?" That's a great quote and it's apropos for this story. In the summer of 1982, Kathy and I along with our friends, Bonnie and Hank, went to Fire Island Pines for the weekend. I didn't know anything about this community, but when we got there, I found out that this was a gay community. Everyone there was overtly gay and everyone looked like they were having a great time. We were the only straight people there!

It was raining Saturday afternoon and I was bored. I walked to town by myself to get a newspaper. Walking towards me was a guy that I recognized from my office building. I had never spoken to him but now we greeted each other and kept walking. I thought to myself, *Wow, I never thought that he was gay.*

As I walked, I realized that he was probably thinking the same thing about me — that I was a gay man!

I had learned my lesson about judging people.

GYM DANDY

LL OF MY life, I have loved being active and athletic. As a yout' (from *My Cousin Vinny*), I played basketball and I jogged; as an adult, I play tennis and I walk.

In the old days, I hated to go to the gym. My reason for hating to go to the gym is evident. In the early 80s, when we moved to Great Neck, I joined a modern gym near the Great Neck train station. Since it was so convenient, I went early in the morning, took a shower there, and got on the train to go to work. Or, if I chose, I could go to the gym after work and then go home. Most of the time, I chose not to go to the gym at all! I had a hard time pushing myself to go, but I tried to do it once a week.

I was at the gym one morning, running on the treadmill and watching television on the big screen in front of me. I remember that there was a commercial for Exxon that showed a car speeding on a curving road. I watched the car take some hairpin turns, and suddenly I was on the floor. I took a hairpin turn and fell off the treadmill!

Everyone rushed to help me, fearing that I had suffered a heart attack. The gym manager asked if I was hurt. Very embarrassed, I thought that the only thing hurt was my feelings!

Hating Exxon, I cut up their credit card and now only use Chevron.

LE PEEP

IN 1982, DR. Tapper, my New Jersey doctor of fifteen years, recommended that I take the G.I. series of tests, only because I had never taken them before. The colonoscopy had not been invented yet, so I was forced to take the barium enema test. The preparation for the colonoscopy is horrible, as is the preparation for the barium test. Without going into lurid detail, the actual barium exam is the worst. But, everything came out okay!

I endured and suffered through this horrible impersonal experience and couldn't wait to go home. Kathy had driven me to the doctor, and since I hadn't eaten breakfast, I was starving. She suggested that we go to a little breakfast/lunch restaurant in Great Neck called *Le Peep*.

Without missing a beat, I said, "They should change the name of the restaurant to *Le POOP!*

Even Kathy laughed.

I WANT RIBS!

M Y FAMILY LOVES barbecue ribs.
Ribs may not have been the food recommended by doctors, but, in spite of the medical profession, my family still loved barbecue ribs!

There was a great rib takeout restaurant located in Delray Beach. One evening, accompanied by my ten-year-old daughter, Vanessa, we drove there to pick up a large order of ribs, enough to feed five hungry Karp family members. The takeout counter was really crowded with salivating barbecue connoisseurs. Suddenly, the proprietor, certainly not an English major, made an important announcement, "Sorry folks, we ain't got no more ribs. We only got catfish!"

A gentleman, standing behind me became enraged. This Harvard graduate student screamed, "I doesn't want any f——g catfish, I want f——-g ribs!"

From his pocket, he pulled a large gun and started to waive it all around! I grabbed Vanessa's hand, and we sprinted out of the restaurant, meaning that we would not have catfish for dinner.

To appease the medical profession, that night we had salad and yogurt!

GET A JOB!

THE U.S. GOVERNMENT says that a worker is supposed to retire at age sixty-five. I proved the government wrong because I retired early — at age forty-five. My retirement was short-lived as I went back to work soon thereafter. I proved the government wrong again as I finally retired late — at age seventy-five.

I came home from work that day in 1984 and told the family that I had left my business after twenty plus years and that I was officially retired. I had considered this life-changing event for a long time. Even though I felt terrific about this decision, my family was taken aback. My eleven-year-old daughter Vanessa asked, "Does that mean that there will be no more wads of cash on the dresser? Does this mean that we're poor?"

I reassured everybody that things would be fine (I hoped). Now I had to decide just what I wanted to with the rest of my life. I received several phone calls from owners of garment businesses, who were my competition, asking whether I wanted to join their companies. Politely, I said no to all of them, as I absolutely did not want to return to that volatile business.

I thought about going back to school and getting a graduate degree, an MBA. I had always wanted to be a doctor, but the idea of medical school and the time and effort required would be rough. Being a lawyer intrigued me, but knowing that law school was really hard frightened me. What would happen if I failed? How would this look to my children? So, I had many choices with what to do with the rest of my life.

Someone told me that if I took an aptitude test, I would be guided to the profession that best suited me. I investigated and found an organization that specialized in aptitude tests and I had a series of interviews that were very interesting.

The advisor asked me a terrific question. If I had three choices to be or to do anything that I wanted, what would I choose? I answered:

1) I would want to be George Karp, playing tennis in the finals at Wimbledon.

2) I would want to be George Karp, playing shortstop for the New York Mets.

3) I would want to be George Karp, being the best person, the best husband, and the best father that I could be.

The advisor applauded my answers. Then she gave me a series of tests that took forever. When I returned the next week, she had the results of the tests.

Basically, the tests revealed that:

1) I should not be a farmer.

2) I should not be a beautician.

3) I should not be a shortstop for the Mets.

4) I should be a businessman.

I guess I knew this all along, that I was best suited for a career in business. I ended my retirement a few months later, becoming involved in real estate. Ultimately, I became a vice president at Helmsley Spear, the giant real estate company in Manhattan. Moving to Florida in 1992, I became a financial advisor for AG Edwards, and ultimately became a Certified Financial Planner. In 2003, I joined Barry Kaye, the largest seller of life insurance in the country, and I became an integral part of his team until I retired in 2014.

Interestingly, I worked longer in my post-retirement years (thirty), then I did in my pre-retirement years (twenty-two). I really screwed up the government's retirement numbers.

Sorry, President Trump!

MY BASEBALL CAREER

A s a boy, I had a few aspirations regarding baseball.

a) I would have liked to play shortstop for the Brooklyn Dodgers.

b) I would have liked to be the radio announcer for the Brooklyn Dodgers.

c) I would have liked to be an executive with the Brooklyn Dodgers.

Obviously, none of these aspirations panned out especially since the Dodgers moved to Los Angeles. But, I did become close to becoming an executive with the New York Mets.

A neighbor of mine Patrick worked for his father-in-law in the real estate business. At dinner one evening, Patrick told me that he was invited to the bar mitzvah of the son of the owner of the New York Mets, Fred Wilpon. He told me that he was very friendly with Mr. Wilpon — then I had an idea!

I had just retired from my business in the spring of 1984, and I was not sure what I wanted to do with the rest of my life. But now, the idea of a career in baseball was intriguing. I told Patrick that if he could speak to his friend Mr. Wilpon about me, I would be forever indebted to him. I said, "Tell Mr. Wilpon that you have a friend age forty-five, who has just retired from a successful business career. He knows more about baseball than anyone, and he would love to work in the front office of the Mets. He would be willing to work for no salary for six months.

If the Mets would like him and conversely, if he would like the Mets, then after six months a deal could be struck."

Patrick said of course he would speak to his friend for me, and I waited each day for a phone call from Patrick. Finally, he called me with the bad news. Patrick told me that his father-in-law was deeply insulted that he was not invited to the Wilpon bar mitzvah. The father-in-law told Patrick that if he went to the bar mitzvah, he should start looking for another job.

Since Patrick and his family liked to eat three meals a day, his job was obviously paramount.

Patrick's friendship with the owner of the Mets had struck out!

Strike Three — there went my baseball career!

TENNIS ANYONE?

MEMORIAL DAY IN 1984 was very memorable to me. We were in Westhampton for the weekend and the weather was cool and drizzly. I played tennis in the morning and I felt that I had pulled a muscle in my calf. I had another match in the afternoon and it was much cooler and rainier. Without warming up, I began to play, and on the first point, I ran back to cover a lob.

I heard something snap in my leg. I thought that someone had thrown a racket at me and hit me in the leg. I went down hard and in pain. Fortunately for me, my partner was a doctor who examined my leg. He was confident that I hadn't ruptured my Achilles tendon (that would have required surgery). He thought that I had torn my plantaris tendon and he was absolutely right.

On the next court, play had stopped and everyone was crowded around me. One of the players, Mike, a WWII veteran, always wore white long pants and had a noticeable limp. What he did then was unbelievable. He rolled up his pant's leg and displayed his prosthetic leg. He took off the leg and started to waive it all around. He shouted, to make me laugh, "George, you think that you have problems? I've got a f——-g wooden leg!"

A few months later, I had recovered and was playing tennis one Sunday morning at my club in Long Island City. I was telling one of the members, Leon, that I had hurt my hamstring.

He gave me sage advice by saying, "Jews don't have hamstrings. They have pastrami strings!"

***

My friend Mike told me that he was buying the tennis club in Westhampton and would I be interested in investing with him. I was not thinking about the club as an investment, but rather the fact that as an owner, I conceivably could get into better games. I agreed and now I was a part owner of a tennis club. When I demanded getting into better games, Mario, the head pro who was now my employee told me, "George, you talk better than you play!" That comment set me back about ten years!

***

When I moved to Woodfield Country Club in 2005, I started to take lessons from Laurent, the head tennis Pro. He must have known Mario, because he told me, "George, you have very good hands but you have very bad feet!" The tennis pros must have a conspiracy against me!

I have a tennis friend who has a great strategy. He is notorious for making bad calls and everything close to the line is called *out.* When he played an important club match, early on, he would call *in* everything close to the line. Now the other team totally trusted him and when the match came to its conclusion, every close ball was called *out.* The other team knew that he was an honest man, and they would never question his call.

Smart man, he never lost!

WATERGATE, TEN YEARS LATER

LOOKING AROUND FOR President Nixon, Kathy and I had dinner in 1984 in the restaurant of the infamous Watergate Hotel in Washington DC. The food was great and the prices were greater. Politicians were everywhere and this was the place in Washington DC to be seen. I'm not sure if I was recognized!

Across the spacious room, there was a very strange sight. Three men sitting at a table were eating their dinner, but each person had a napkin draped over his head and face. I thought this was a religious experience for these people, but I didn't know which religion they were honoring. Finally, they finished their meal, removed their napkins, and left the restaurant.

I asked the manager of the restaurant what the heck were those people doing. He told me that they were eating a special pigeon dish and the covered napkin kept the aroma of the bird intact so that they could inhale the special aroma.

Now when I go to a restaurant, I always put a napkin over my head, so I can smell the special aroma of my hamburger!

GEORGE SEGAL LOOK-A-LIKE

KATHY AND I traveled to California in 1984, and we had dinner with her Los Angeles cousins, Gloria and Leonard. They took us to a fancy "shmancy" restaurant in Beverly Hills, where they seemed to know everyone — all Hollywood celebrities. Who came over to our table to greet them, but actor George Segal, who was then at the top of his career. When introduced, we shook hands and he said to me, "You know, we look alike."

I said to him that many people have told me that over the years. And then I said, "What's even more interesting is that I live in Great Neck and that you grew up in Great Neck. I tell shopkeepers that I am you and for years, I have been signing your name on my bills, all over town."

George Segal laughed and told me that I owed him about $10,000!

UNREAL ESTATE

M Y SIX-MONTH RETIREMENT from the garment industry in 1984 was short-lived, as I soon began my career in real estate. I became involved with a Long Island brokerage company and I attempted to sell investment properties. It took a while for me to learn the nuances of real estate, but eventually, I got the hang of it.

My first real deal was the sale of a small shopping center, just north of New York City. The property included a big parcel of land, several stores, and a small two-story office building. Contracts were signed and now the deal was ready to be closed. I went to the closing along with Herb, the president of the company, Schacker Real Estate.

The buyer of the property showed us a letter that he received from the town, telling of the need for an elevator to be installed in the office building. The buyer flatly exclaimed that *he* would not be paying the cost of installing the elevator and the shaft. The seller of the property adamantly said that *he* would not be paying for the elevator and the shaft.

The buyer and seller both looked at us and said that if the deal is to be done, then the broker (ME) would pay the cost of installing the elevator and the shaft. The president and I went outside, had a quick conversation and decided that in order to keep the deal intact, we would have to pay for the elevator and the shaft. What once looked like a fat commission for me, now was just skin and bones.

The elevator should be known as the *"Schacker Shaft"* because we got shafted!

A few months later, I learned that a shopping center near my office on Long Island might be available for sale. I drove there to inspect the property and to take a few pictures. The shopping center was in a very bad neighborhood, and it was really dilapidated. I drove around and noticed a group of young boys hanging around one of the vacant stores. These boys did not look like Ivy Leaguers and soon they began to chase after my car. I realized quickly that this was a drug situation, and they thought that I was either a buyer or a seller, not a real estate broker!

I drove to the far end of the property and got out of my car to take pictures. Here they come again! I jumped back into my car and took off just before they could overtake me. This was definitely not a property that I would consider showing to clients.

The boys did not do any business that day, and neither did I!

CARROTS & PEAS

S OME WOMEN LOVE to cook; other women love not to cook.
So there we were, the Karp family, one evening in 1985 at the Scobee Diner, a local eatery, of blessed memory. I happen to love diners and their extensive menus because the food is usually terrific. I have a theory that if fat people go to a restaurant, that means the food is plentiful and good. Fat people went to the Scobee Diner!

Everyone had ordered their meal and now it was my turn. I asked the waitress what were the vegetable side dishes, and she ran off a long list of vegetables, including spinach, broccoli, brussels sprouts, asparagus, carrots and peas, etc. I ordered carrots and peas. She looked at me and said, "Why order that? You can get carrots and peas at home."

I countered with, "My dear waitress, if I could get carrots and peas at home, then I wouldn't be eating here!"

My girls laughed, but Kathy gave me a dirty look!

SQUEEGEE TERRORISM

IN THE MID-1980s, New York City was afflicted by a new and different kind of terrorism — *Squeegee Terrorism.*

The terrorists were usually homeless men and their weapons were a squeegee and a bucket of dirty soapy water. These men created terror in the streets to motorists attempting to enter the Midtown Tunnel. Their attack locations were in the blocks from East 30th Street to East 40th Street, along First Avenue and Second Avenue.

These *soldiers of soap* would approach a car, usually stuck in traffic, and slather its windshield with a torrent of soapy water. The antagonist would stick his hand into the car and politely demand money from the startled driver. When the driver would surrender and cough up some change, the terrorist would squeegee the soapy water from the windshield. If the driver refused to give money, he then would have the soapiest windshield in Manhattan.

One evening, driving home from work, I encountered a squeegee terrorist. Before I could blink, my windshield was covered with a soapy liquid. Since these men had no toilet facilities, I wondered what liquid was in the bucket.

I reached in my pocket for a dollar bill and found that I only had five and ten dollar bills. I certainly was not going to give this gentleman a five dollar tip. In my ashtray, I kept tokens to use for the tunnel toll; each token was worth one dollar and fifty cents.

I was not happy parting with a buck and a half token but obviously, I had no choice. I gave the man the token and he gave me a dirty look.

In a nasty tone he said, "What am I going to do with a token? I don't even have a car."

"Kind sir," I replied, "with all the money that you earned today, you can buy a Cadillac tomorrow."

I drove off with the cleanest windshield in Manhattan!

ALMOST MUGGED

EVERY SEPTEMBER, ON the Tuesday before the Great Neck schools reopened for my kids, we went to the US Open tennis tournament in Flushing Meadow, Queens. The year was 1985, and the tennis that afternoon was great. The last day match that we saw was over at about 8 o'clock and by then, all of the people attending the night matches were already in their seats. There is a long boardwalk outside the Tennis Center that goes over the Grand Central Parkway that connects with the parking lot at Shea Stadium, then the home of the Mets. My car was parked in the lot, so we had to cross the boardwalk. Normally, the boardwalk was crowded with people. That night because the evening tennis had already started, the boardwalk was dark and deserted.

I was walking with Heather and Vanessa, while Kathy was up ahead with Jennifer. Being slightly paranoid, I looked behind me and saw two big guys walking quickly towards us. I was nervous!

The men passed us and purposely, I now slowed up. Finally, we reached the other side and I saw and heard a commotion. I was thinking that maybe these guys were involved in a robbery or a murder or even something worse.

I heard someone yell, "Hey Darryl" as we approached the crowd. Darryl Strawberry, star outfielder for the Mets was signing autographs.

My claim to fame is that I was almost mugged by Darryl Strawberry!

NOT-YET PRESIDENT TRUMP

THIS IS A humorous tale about our president, Donald Trump.

Thirty years before his election, my sixteen-year-old daughter Heather, and I were going to spend a few days *father and daughter bonding.* Our plan was to drive to Washington DC to see the sights of the capital. We were in the midst of a heat wave, and as I was driving, the thought of a sizzling Washington DC started to turn me off. Going south on the New Jersey Turnpike, I posed the question, "Instead of hot Washington DC, how about going to the cool beach in Atlantic City?"

Heather immediately said yes. I figured that if I had offered Antarctica as an alternative, she would have said yes! As we drove to Atlantic City, Heather asked, "Dad, where are we going to stay?"

I saw a big billboard that said "Trump Plaza" and I pointed to the sign and told her that it looked like a nice place to spend a few days. When we arrived, the hotel looked jammed. We had no reservation, but I figured that I would take a shot. The desk clerk told me that no rooms were available, so I asked to see the manager. Again, the manager said that he did not have a room for me. I took him to the side and told him that I was a personal friend of Donald Trump. I said, "When I call Don tomorrow morning and tell him that I could not get a room in his hotel, he will be very upset."

Fearful of possible consequences, the manager said, "Right this way, sir. I hope that you will be happy with your suite."

In disbelief, Heather asked me if I knew Donald Trump. I told her,

"Well, sort of. Last year on a flight from Florida, we were on the same plane. Waiting for our luggage, I smiled at him and he smiled at me. So, we're buddies!"

Heather liked this part: That evening, we were eating in the buffet restaurant. The waitress was serving mashed potatoes, and she asked me if I would like some. I answered, "Just a drop."

I inadvertently pulled my plate away and the scoop of mashed potatoes fell to the floor.

I told Heather, "Well, it was just a drop."

Thirty years later, Heather is still laughing!

BOCA WEST PANDEMONIUM

I N OLD DETECTIVE movies, they say that the criminal always returns to the scene of the crime. But I'm not a criminal and Boca West certainly is not a crime scene.

We owned an apartment in Boca West for three years in the early '80s, but it was too small, and we rarely used it — so we sold it. But the family missed Florida and each Christmas, we returned to Boca West by renting a condo there.

It was Christmas 1986, and we left the cold of New York for the warmth of Florida. We took a late flight that was delayed, and until we picked up our rental car, we didn't get to Boca West until after midnight. The apartment was hot and stuffy and all the lights were out.

"Turn on the air-conditioning," everyone said loudly.

It was dark and I couldn't find the control for the air-conditioning. But, I did find three buttons that I thought controlled the lights, the fan, and the air-conditioning so I pressed each one. When one of the girls found a flashlight, I realized that I had made a terrible mistake — I had pressed the wrong buttons. Within five minutes, there was pandemonium outside!

A fire engine, two police cars, and three EMS vehicles were outside our apartment — all with flashing lights. The firemen had their axes out and were ready to knock down the front door. The police had their guns drawn looking for intruders. The EMS workers were rolling their stretchers ready for heart attack victims. Our new neighbors, in their ugly pajamas, were outside trying to figure out what had happened.

I apologized to the fire department, the police department, the EMS department, and all of my new neighbors, and told them all that I hoped they were not inconvenienced.

I was not the most popular person that season in Boca West!

MY HITCH- HIKING ADVENTURE

I REMEMBER JANUARY 1987 very well. I had hurt my back and the pain from sciatica was killing me. The Long Island Rail Road was on strike, and it was very difficult traveling to the city. Every morning Kathy drove me to Flushing and I took the subway to Manhattan; in the evening she picked me up in Flushing and we drove home to Great Neck.

One afternoon, a sudden snowstorm hit New York City and driving was a problem. I told Kathy not to drive to Flushing; I would take a taxi home to Great Neck (there was no such thing as Uber). Except, there were no taxis, my feet were wet, my head was wet and cold, and my back hurt. Other than that, everything was fine!

I found a small Army and Navy store near the Flushing station that was doing more business that day than it had done in all of the previous year. The owner probably changed every price tag to double what it had been the day before. I bought a pair of rubbers that were about five sizes too large and a wool cap that reeked of mothballs!

My plan was to walk to Northern Boulevard, a main thoroughfare, and if I couldn't get a taxi, I would hitch a ride to Great Neck. Not a taxi on the road! As I was trying to hitch a ride, every driver looked at me and kept going. After a half hour of total rejection, I looked in a store window and realized why nobody would stop for me. My new wool cap, pulled down so that my ears were protruding, made me look like a total idiot! I took off the mothball-smelling cap, stepped into the street, and the first car stopped and drove me to Great Neck.

That was quite a night!
And, I still have the cap. And it still smells.

SENIOR CITIZENS

P RESIDENTS' DAY MEANT no work for me, and on that February Monday, Kathy and I drove to Westhampton to inspect our condo. Driving back, I spotted a new multiplex theater on the Long Island Expressway.

"I haven't been to the movies in the daytime in years," I said. "Let's catch a flick."

At the ticket booth, there was a sign : *"Adults $8. Seniors $5. (Must be over 65 with identification)."*

I had just turned forty-eight, and I looked and felt young that day; Kathy was a youthful-looking forty-four.

The gum-chewing girl selling tickets was about sixteen and I wanted to play a joke on her.

"I want to buy a senior ticket because I'm seventy-two, but I have no identification with me."

She eyed me cautiously, and then said, " Okay, that's ten dollars for two senior tickets."

I was happy because I saved six bucks.

Kathy was furious because the young girl thought that my forty-four-year old wife looked like the young girl's grandmother!

BRING BACK THE CZAR

D URING THE SUMMER of 1987, Kathy and I had the opportunity
to travel to the Union of Soviet Socialist Republics. For the
uninformed, the U.S.S.R. (the Soviet Union) disintegrated in
1991 and evolved into fifteen independent republics. But in 1987, we
witnessed the end of communism as we visited Moscow, Leningrad
(now St. Petersburg) in Russia, and three cities in Uzbekistan —
Tashkent, Bukhara, and Samarkand.

For most of my life, the United States and the Soviet Union were
involved in a Cold War, that at times almost became a hot war. I
wanted to see for myself just what our perpetual enemy looked like.
For two weeks we traveled the country and I became more and more
disappointed. To me, the Soviet Union looked like a paper tiger, with
nothing for us to fear. I felt that either by revolution or evolution, the
Soviet Union was going to change. The evolutionary change took place
in just four years.

Moscow, a huge city, was sad to behold. The large stores had no
merchandise, the wide avenues had no cars, the food was terrible, and
all of the people looked like they were ready to cry. The biggest tourist
attraction was Lenin's tomb, where thousands of people stood in line
daily to see the remains of Comrade Lenin. When we finally got in, I
was reprimanded by a Soviet policeman who told me to take my hands
out of my pockets and to zip up my jacket. We saw Mr. Lenin lying
there, and I thought that he moved!

We viewed the Kremlin, St. Basil's Cathedral, and Red Square. We saw the famous GUM department store, but there was nothing to buy, except vodka, that the Russian people drank instead of water.

In Moscow, we witnessed the riches of the Czars. We saw the palaces and all the wealth of the Russian rulers. We saw the luxurious coach that Katherine the Great, Ivan the Terrible, and Nicholas the Mediocre traveled in. One coach was encrusted with diamonds and rubies and other fabulous jewels, while I'm sure the peasants of that era were hungry. But considering the state of the Soviet Union in 1987, some wise Russian comrade should have held up a sign saying — *"Bring back the Czar!"*

This was the time of the "refuseniks," where many people, mostly Jewish, were trying to leave Russia, but could not. We visited some of these people who lived in tiny apartments and many of them were sick. We "shlepped" diapers, food, and other items all around Moscow, distributing them to the refuseniks. Getting around the city by taxicab represented a problem because the few taxis would not stop for passengers. We were informed before we left home: buy a carton of Marlboro cigarettes, because the way to get a taxi to stop would be to flash a red pack of Marlboro's. This strategy actually worked!

Supposedly, the hotel rooms were bugged. Every night I said very loudly, " Moscow is really great. We are having the best time."

Bottom line, we were not arrested!

Since there was nothing to buy in Moscow, there were no shopping sprees, and we went to the local ice cream store one afternoon. There was a very long line and we waited to be served. Strangely, there were no signs posted on the wall telling of the different flavors of ice cream. We learned that this was not Baskin-Robbins and the thirty-one flavors. There was one flavor ice cream and the color was gray. I have to admit that it was pretty good. I think that they called it *"Commy Garcia!"*

***

Uzbekistan was really something else. The people were descended from the Mongol hordes and really looked different. I have great pictures of some of these people. Other than being communists, they really had nothing in common with the Moscow Russians. We flew from Uzbekistan to Leningrad in the middle of the night, for some weird Soviet reason. We got to Leningrad about 5 a.m. and our bus from the airport suddenly stopped. It stopped because the drawbridge over the river was up and it stayed up all night. The operator of the drawbridge didn't come to work until 8 a.m. and nobody else could lower the drawbridge. There was a huge traffic jam but I guess that it happened every night, and the Russians did not care. The Czar would not be happy!

Leningrad, from afar, was a great-looking city, but up close it was dirty, and looked like it was falling apart. We stayed in a new hotel that was dilapidated, on the Baltic Sea. The beach was littered with garbage and nobody picked it up. One morning, walking along the beach, we noticed a man sunning himself, lying on a lounge. Getting closer, we realized that the lounge was really a big mound of garbage!

But the museums, especially the Summer Palace, were spectacular and the artwork was unbelievable. The Winter Palace holds the Hermitage Museum, with so many great pieces of art. Touring the very crowded museum, Kathy and I lost each other. In one room, there was a crowd of people and some of them were screaming. I got closer and saw a fat woman kicking another woman.

That *other* woman was Kathy Karp. The fight was broken up quickly and Kathy did not know what came over the Russian lady. Someone said that the other woman kicked field goals for the Leningrad Lions!

Before we left New York, a dentist friend who had been to Leningrad gave me the best advice. He told me *not* to drink the water in the hotel or in a restaurant and *not* to buy bottled water. He said the only thing to drink was Pepsi-Cola and to brush our teeth only with Pepsi. This seemed crazy, but he said that the water in Leningrad was loaded with sulfur, which will make one's teeth discolored. We followed his advice, but other people on the trip did not listen. On the flight home, everyone had black teeth except Kathy and me.

I've been brushing my teeth with Pepsi-Cola ever since!

MY PAL REGIS

FTER WE HAD sold our Great Neck house in 1991, we rented an apartment in a new building on East 88th Street, in Manhattan. One evening around Christmas time, I saw a crowd of people standing on the corner of First Avenue and East 88th Street. They were filming a new movie, *Night and the City* with Robert DeNiro, and everyone wanted a glimpse of this superstar.

Standing next to me in the crowd was a man I recognized from television — Regis Philbin. I started a conversation with him, and he told me that he had a small part in the film. He laughed when I told him that I would see the movie just to view him.

The next night, the family went to see the new Barbra Streisand movie, *Prince of Tides*. Guess who was sitting right behind me — Regis Philbin. He remembered me, shook my hand, and I introduced him to the Karp family.

My kids were impressed!

GIMME A "W"

WHEN I MOVED to Boca Raton in 1992, it gave me the opportunity to go to a Walmart store.

I had never been to a Walmart before because there were none in the New York area. The novelty soon wore off and quickly I was back to Bloomingdale's. The most interesting thing about Walmart was that when the store opened at about 9 a.m., a pep rally began. The manager yelled, "Gimme a 'W,' gimme an 'A,'" until Walmart is spelled out by all of the employees. It was similar to the cheerleaders at a high school football game!

Recently, I passed a Walmart store, and I went in to look around for a bargain. I was in the drug aisle, standing next to a Haitian saleslady. A woman about seventy-five or eighty started to ask the clerk a question. "Where can I find a stool softener?" the customer asked.

The Walmart saleslady looked at her strangely. The puzzled saleslady responded, "What's a stool softener?"

The customer was now getting frustrated and embarassed, waving her arms all around, and said, "You know, it makes you go to the bathroom. It's not for me, it's for my mother (Who certainly would have to be over 100!)."

The sales lady thought for a while and finally said, "Maybe you should try the furniture department!"

I wonder if the furniture department is next to the restroom!

THE AX MURDERER

ABOUT TO BE divorced, I came to Florida in June 1992. Not a happy camper, I rented a nice apartment, but sadly, for the first time in my life, I was alone. I didn't really know anyone, so I had to start my social life from scratch. My sister Arlene had an old friend, Joni, who lived nearby and was delighted to hear that I was coming to live in Boca. She arranged "singles parties," and she had a Rolodex filled with information about eligible single ladies. She called me often, giving me countless phone numbers of single women who wanted to meet single men.

Joni was having a party in a restaurant one Sunday evening and invited me to attend. She told me that there would be many great-looking women at the party. She lied. I walked around the restaurant, eyeing all the ladies, and I was not impressed.

The best of a bad lot was sitting at the bar, and I started a conversation with her. Actually, she was a nice lady, not bad looking, and very intelligent. When the party was over, I offered to drive her home. She thought about it and said, "Yes, but you could be an axe murderer!"

"Do I look like an axe murderer? I'm just a nice Jewish boy from Brooklyn!"

I drove her home and asked her out for the next Saturday night.

Always a subtle practical joker, I knew that I had to do something funny for her. Saturday afternoon, I went to the local Kmart store and in the sporting goods department, I purchased a big hatchet for twenty-five dollars. I propped the big axe in the passenger seat of my car.

That evening, I rang her bell and said, "Here's the axe murderer!"

I opened the car door for her, and when she saw the hatchet, it blew her mind. She laughed for fifteen minutes and said that this was the funniest thing she had ever seen. She called her father who was in the hospital, told him the story, and he laughed so hard that his stitches broke.

Not being a lumberjack and having no need for the axe, I returned it to Kmart the next day, and got my twenty-five bucks back!

THESE SHOES ARE MEANT FOR DRIVIN'

ARRIVING IN BOCA Raton in 1992, I took a walking tour of downtown Boca one day. I came upon a small shoe store and bought a great pair of driving shoes. After wearing them for a few weeks, I noticed that they were getting very worn on the heels of both shoes. I brought them back to the store anticipating an exchange or a refund. The owner was adamant and told me that the shoes were meant for driving, not walking. I guess that he had not listened to the Nancy Sinatra song!

My argument was that I had to walk to my car before I could drive it. Guess what — I lost the argument!

MY GRANDMOTHER'S FRIEND

RIGHT AFTER I moved to Florida in 1992, I joined a local tennis club. I played doubles with a nice fellow Richard and we became quite friendly. Richard told me that he knew a pretty lady that he wanted me to meet. Not knowing too many people locally, I quickly called her and made a date to meet her at a quiet restaurant in Boca. She told me that she was blonde and she would wear a red dress.

I got to the restaurant early and eagerly waited at the bar for my date. A blonde lady with a red dress came in, looked around, and sat down at the bar. I looked at her closely and saw that she must have been twenty years older than me. She might have been a classmate of my grandmother!

I was about to approach this elderly lady when a younger blonde lady with a red dress came into the restaurant, who obviously was my date. We had dinner, but I was not too impressed with this lady and there would not be a second date.

Bottom line, I would have been better off with my grandmother's friend!

VOODOO LADY

P LAYING TENNIS AT the club that I had joined, just after I moved to Boca Raton, I became friendly with another one of the members. His wife's best friend was a pretty single lady and my new friend thought that I might like her. Her name was Leslie and I called her. It's a small world because she grew up in Manhattan Beach, right next to Brighton Beach; she went to Lincoln and I knew her cousin.

I took Leslie out to dinner, but I did not recognize her at all from our high school days. Then she told me the weirdest thing, "I have a picture of you and me at a party together."

This was impossible, I told her. "I have a great memory, and I remember every day of my life. I remember every party that I have ever gone to, and I remember every girl that I ever dated. *I do not* remember you. You must have a picture of someone else who resembles me, but it just can't be me!"

I took Leslie home and she retrieved a picture from the night table next to her bed. This was getting really weird! The small picture WAS OF ME, when I was about eighteen, with a young Leslie! I just couldn't believe the picture! More important, why did this lady keep this thirty-five-year-old photo next to her bed? Maybe she believed in voodoo and for thirty-five years, she stuck pins in me. Maybe every headache and toothache and earache that I've had for thirty-five years was because of her voodoo pins!

Leslie told me that the party was a sweet sixteen party for her cousin, and her cousin in New York still had all the pictures of that party. She said she would contact her cousin who would then send her the big picture of us together. Leslie called me a week later and told me that she had received the big picture from her cousin. I immediately went to her apartment to view the mystery photo!

It was a large photo with about fifty people in the picture and then I remembered the party. Yes, I spotted myself standing next to Leslie, but on the other side of me was Paula, who was my date for the party. Standing next to Leslie, was her date, a classmate of mine. My friend Harvey was standing nearby with his girlfriend, Pat. Again, this was really weird!

I related this strange story to Harvey, and he gave me some good advice. "Ditch this lady!"

I certainly did!

THE THREE POINT SHOT

GOING TO THE gym, as previously explained, was never one of my favorite things. Truth be told, I hated it!

When I moved to Florida, I joined a local gym and pushed myself to go twice a week. The gym had a nice basketball court, and after my workout, I would shoot some hoops, all by myself. In the NBA, at this time, the three point shot was becoming more and more important. NBA players would try the three point shot from far out and at best, convert one out of three attempts.

In the good old days, when I last played basketball (and not very well), shooting from far out was unheard of. So now, I started to practice shooting these long heaves, and of course, I was very unsuccessful. Finally, after a few weeks, I made my first three pointer. I was ecstatic! Each time I went to the gym, I practiced shooting, and then one day I hit two in a row.

One magic morning a few weeks later, I cannot explain what happened. Unbelievably, I scored five long shots in a row! I figured that I was now ready to play for the Miami Heat!

I think I phoned everyone I knew in New York to tell them about my unbelievable exploit. My lawyer friend Stanley, who knew I was not much of a basketball player, could not believe it. He asked me, "Do you have any witnesses?"

When I told him there were no witnesses, he calmly said, "I do not believe you" and hung up on me!

My basketball confidence shattered, I don't think that I ever scored a three pointer again!

MEMORIES OF RITA

Rita Bari and I started dating in 1993, and for Valentine's Day 1994, I went shopping to buy her a small present. We weren't really serious yet, and so I didn't want to get her a serious gift (for serious money). I went into a jewelry store in the Town Center Mall in Boca looking for a trinket. I met a client of mine who was a very heavy hitter! He told me that he had just bought his wife a terrific gift, a string of pearls that was only one twenty-eight.

I thought to myself that one hundred-twenty-eight dollars represented a good deal that fit into my budget, so my client asked the salesgirl to show me the string of pearls that he had bought.

I started to get suspicious when the sales girl unlocked the safe to get the pearls. They were beautiful and I nervously asked the price.

"They are only *one hundred twenty-eight thousand dollars*", the happy salesgirl said, subconsciously counting her commission money.

Before I fainted, I told the girl that I was looking for something more elaborate, and I ran out of the store!

***

After dating for a long while because of divorce complications, we finally decided to get married. Rita and I were planning our wedding, and I wanted to buy a new suit for the occasion.

I settled on a beautiful beige suit that looked and fit just great. The store had many suits in stock and some were pretty wild. I looked at a bright yellow suit and thought that I could play a great trick on Rita. I borrowed the suit and told the salesman that I would bring it back the next day.

I came home and showed Rita the bright yellow suit. She knew that I had very good taste, but she couldn't believe what I had selected. When she started to cry, I knew that I had gone too far.

"Only kidding," I said and she was totally relieved.

***

Visiting Vanessa and her family in California in 2004, I was given tickets to see the Los Angeles Dodgers play the San Francisco Giants. We sat behind the dugout and saw Barry Bonds hit one of his many home runs. At one point, the Dodgers third baseman made a great throw to first base to get the runner. Rita asked me if I could throw like that from third base to first base.

I replied, "At my age, from third base I can't even see first base!"

I think she understood.

***

My son-in-law Darryl was celebrating his fortieth birthday in 2009, and a big party was held in Napa. We flew to San Francisco and rented a car to explore the area. I wanted to drive south from Napa to Los Angeles on Big Sur, and take great pictures with my new camera.

Rita had never encountered Big Sur and she didn't know what she was in for. She always complained about my driving, saying that I drove too slow, just like an old lady. She started to get really nervous on the hairpin turns, and she was holding on tight. "You are driving too fast, can you please slow down!", she shrieked.

I responded, "You always tell me that I drive too slow, make up your mind."

The "old lady" driver was only going twenty-five mph!

***

One morning at 4:00 a.m., I stumbled out of bed into the bathroom. When I came out at 4:02 a.m., much to my amazement, the bed was made. I asked Rita what was going on and why did she make the bed.

"I thought that you were up for the day," she answered.

"It's the middle of the night," I said. "The birds aren't even up yet."

"I'm sorry dear," she said and we both laughed ourselves back to sleep!

***

Rita and I loved to go to the movies on Saturday nights. Once in 2010, we spent the evening at Shadowwood in Boca, seeing a movie so memorable that I don't remember its name. When the movie was over, Rita waited for me while I visited the men's room.

The men's room was crowded and I had to wait in line. Finally, when I came out, Rita was annoyed and asked what took me so long.

I answered, "You wouldn't believe it. The man in front of me was talking to his prostate!"

She laughed so hard and told me that I had made her Saturday night complete, even with a lousy movie!

These are just a few memories of Rita, many more are still in my heart.

Rita and George — Wedding Day — 2000

Rita and George, 2006.

THE BELLY ACHE

IN THE FALL of 1994, my daughter Vanessa was a senior at the University of Wisconsin. She planned a weekend trip to visit the old man in Florida, and Rita and I really looked forward to it. However, my stomach was hurting me for a few days, and of course I did nothing about it. I told Vanessa about this when I picked her up at the airport, and she insisted that I see a doctor. A friend gave me the name of a G.I. specialist, Dr. C., and he was able to squeeze me in for a late afternoon appointment.

He also squeezed my stomach and told me, "You have appendicitis, my friend."

I could not believe this diagnosis and I was certainly not his friend.

Dr. C. advised me to go to Boca Raton Regional Hospital, check in, and he would contact the surgeon, Dr. P. Other then when I was born, I had never been in a hospital before, on my account. Rita and Vanessa rushed to the hospital, and when Vanessa saw me lying in the emergency room, she started to cry. I was not a happy camper!

The surgeon, Dr. P., came to see me, and he was convinced that my appendix had to be removed, of course by him. By now, it was almost midnight and thankfully Dr. P. told me that he was tired, and he would do the operation at 8 a.m. To say that I had a sleepless night would be an understatement.

Daybreak arrived and I was nervous about my scheduled procedure. I poked my stomach and felt that it was not hurting as much as the day before. I was hooked to an IV so I got out of bed gingerly and decided to walk the halls to see if my stomach still hurt. I walked faster and started to jog, still attached to the IV machine. The nurses and other patients stared in disbelief to see a man hooked an to IV machine running down the hallway!

When Dr. P. and Dr. C. arrived, I told them that I was feeling better and maybe the operation wasn't necessary. They looked disappointed, maybe thinking about their lost fees, and told me that I was just being "macho." They ordered some tests and x-rays for me, which were a pain in the tush, and when the results came in, they were really disappointed. Both doctors said the results were inconclusive, and they would *not* do the operation that morning.

But, they warned me that since they were sure that I did have appendicitis, I would be back in the hospital within the next few days. I figured that I would take my chances and ultimately, I was right.

The hospital soon released me, and I could not wait to get out of there. Rita brought me an old sweatshirt and pajama bottoms with a broken elastic to wear. The hospital was sending a wheelchair for me, and then I could be formally released. I told Rita, " I am out of here, now. Where did you park?"

I ran down the stairs, without shoes into the parking lot. However, there was a carnival going on in the parking lot, and now hundreds of people saw this crazy, barefoot man, clutching his pajamas with the broken elastic, running across the field looking for his car!

It was a funny sight, and I am sure that when Vanessa told everyone at the University of Wisconsin, all had a good laugh!

Bottom line, I did not have appendicitis, and Drs. C. and P. were just scalpel happy. I think that I just ate a bad turkey sandwich.

WILT WAS THE BEST

My friend Ken invited me to play tennis one morning in 1995, at his club, the Boca Hotel. We played, we had lunch, and then we just hung around the pool in the afternoon. Lying on a lounge nearby, was a large or should I say very large, African-American man. I immediately recognized this person — he was Wilt Chamberlain!

I always enjoyed talking to celebrities so I approached his lounge. I apologized to him for disturbing him, and said, " I just wanted to say hello. I'm from New York and I'm an old-time Knick fan. I saw you play at the Garden so many times. I always rooted against you, but I want you to know that I always thought you were the best!"

He sat up, shook my hand, told me it was nice to meet me, and said, "Thank you very much for your kind words."

In my opinion, Wilt Chamberlain was the best basketball player of all time. He once scored 100 points in a game, a record that will never be equaled. One year, he averaged 50 points per game along with 25 rebounds — truly unbelievable numbers.

Wilt Chamberlain died suddenly in 1999 at age sixty-three. I'm very glad that I had the opportunity to speak with the greatest basketball player, ever!

MY BIRTHDAY PRESENT

LORIDA ATLANTIC UNIVERSITY, FAU, is a great place for senior citizens in Boca Raton. They have a special school, Lifelong Learning Society, that offers many different and varied classes for retired people. I have been going there long before I retired in 2014 and I love it.

My daughter Jennifer has been a producer at MSNBC for several years and knows many of the anchors and contributors. She knew Walid Phares, who is an expert on Middle Eastern affairs. Walid is a lecturer at FAU, and he told Jennifer that he would be giving a class there tomorrow. Jennifer knew that I would be attending that lecture the next day, which just happened to be my birthday, and she wanted to make me feel special.

The 500-seat auditorium was filled to capacity. Walid started his lecture, but first said, "Can George Karp please stand up?"

Not knowing what was going on and feeling very embarrassed, I stood up. Walid started to sing, "Happy birthday to you" and 500 people joined in singing!

Jennifer gave me a very special birthday present!

THE BEST INVESTMENT

I PLAYED LOTS OF fun tennis while living at Boca Pointe, starting in 1995. We had a big group of players, and I enjoyed playing and socializing with these guys. Everyone had a nickname, and because I always ate a banana before I played, I became known as "Banana George."

After tennis, everyone would sit around and shoot the breeze. The stock market, as well as the weather in Boca, was hot in the 1990s, and all the ersatz Warren Buffetts discussed their killings in the market. It seemed nobody at Boca Pointe ever lost on Wall Street!

My friend Bernie was a funny man, besides being a good tennis player. He married, for the third time, a very, very wealthy woman, who had just inherited a fortune from her late father.

One morning after tennis, the market gurus were discussing their great gains on Wall Street. Bernie took the floor and said, "I know that you guys have made millions in the market. But let me tell you about the greatest investment that was ever made. I invested five dollars in a marriage license, and you know the rest!"

That was one great story!

AL GORE - I'M SORRY

UNBELIEVABLE, BUT TRUE. How could a lifelong liberal like me vote for an ultraconservative candidate like Pat Buchanan! But sadly, I did!

In the 2000 Presidential election, the state of Florida had a terribly confusing ballot. The morning of the election, I knew that I was going to vote for Al Gore for President. I was running late and when I left my house, I did not take my reading glasses with me, which presented a bit of a problem. I squinted at the horizontal two-page ballot and did not realize that Al Gore was on line two on the left side, but on line three on the right side — or something confusing like that. Anyway, I checked the box, for what I thought was a vote for Al Gore, but I soon realized that it was the box for Pat Buchanan. With my pencil, I tried to pull out the "chad," but it only pushed it in deeper and created a "hanging chad."

I wonder how many thousands of Floridians made the same mistake as I did and voted for Pat Buchanan, instead of Al Gore.

President George W. Bush sent me a thank you note, as did Pat Buchanan!

STELLA BY STARLIGHT

M Y FIRST GRANDCHILD was born in Los Angeles in January 2001. My daughter Vanessa and son-in-law Darryl named her Stella Gracie, in honor of my mother, Estelle. Her proud grandpa and Rita rushed to California for the adoration of the infant.

I went to the record store and bought a Frank Sinatra CD that of course had on it, "Stella by Starlight." We played it for the baby, and this was the first music that she had ever heard.

Vanessa asked me a very important question, "What name did I want to be called by the grandchild?"

Darryl's father, whose name was Rich, was a wealthy Los Angeles television executive. I asked Vanessa what Darryl's father was going to be called. She told me, "Grandpa Rich."

I immediately said, "Okay, I'll be Grandpa Poor!"

Both Vanessa and Darryl thought this was hilarious.

About a year later, we were in Vanessa's car, and she asked if Rita and I could watch Stella while she went into the store. Stella was laughing and smiling and then looking for her mother, Stella became sad and teary. I did my best to cheer her up but to no avail. She was now crying hysterically in spite of my funny faces. Finally, Vanessa returned and asked if Stella was okay.

"Oh, sure," I fibbed. "She whimpered a little, but she's just fine!"

One Christmas vacation when Stella was ten and Grandson Jeremy was eight, I got tickets for a local Florida circus. We arrived late, just before intermission, but what little we saw, I thought was terrific. The second part opened and there were clowns, acrobats,and elephants and I loved it. Together the kids said, "Let's go, Grandpa. We're bored!"

Bored — how can anyone be bored at the circus? I was disappointed, but we left.

THE JEWISH BILLY GRAHAM

BARRY KAYE WAS a giant in the life insurance industry. He started his career in the 1960s in Los Angeles and quickly became a huge success. Barry, along with his son Howard, relocated their business to Boca Raton in the late '90s. His first employee in Boca was my wife Rita. At her constant urging, I joined the company in 2003, and soon learned Barry Kaye's unique way of successfully doing life insurance business.

Barry, with this powerful voice, was an inspirational speaker. I told him that he was the Jewish Billy Graham! The company's forte in securing new clients was a series of seminars held every month. Large crowds would come to hear Barry speak at these seminars and many would become clients. One day, Rita and I were driving to a seminar at the Ritz-Carlton Hotel in Manalapan, near Palm Beach. We were late, I was speeding, and I got a ticket on Route A1A. It was my first ticket in years.

The next day, I was driving to a seminar in Naples, Florida, where we always had a large enthusiastic audience. Alligator Alley was the road that crossed from the East coast of Florida to the West Coast. The road was clear and I was doing about eighty. Rita always told me that I drove like an old lady and she couldn't believe that I got a speeding ticket the day before. I spotted a police car on the grass, and it entered the highway behind me. Rita said, "Don't worry, he's not coming after you because you drive too slow."

Famous last words! His flashing lights were on and he soon pulled me over. When the officer got out of the car, I couldn't believe it. The female officer looked like a little girl, about sixteen years old, five feet tall, who should be on her way to high school. I told her that I didn't think that I was speeding, and I hadn't received a ticket in many years. As she looked into my car, she pointed to the yellow ticket on the dashboard that I had received yesterday and she laughed. I asked her how fast was I going and she said ninety-five mph.

I had to think quickly and told her that I was just keeping up with traffic. "How fast was the car in front of me going?" I asked.

She told me that the other car was doing about eighty mph. Now I had her.

"Officer, if the other car was doing eighty and I was doing ninety-five, well, that meant that I would be crashing into the other car," I said.

She realized that I was right, and with that, she told me to drive carefully and have a pleasant day. I gave a big sigh of relief!

***

The morning of the seminar, Barry was in rare form. He must have had a good night because this morning he was really energetic! Everyone appeared to be loving his performance when suddenly one man stood up and shouted, "If I had wanted to go to a circus, I would have gone to Ringling Brothers Barnum and Bailey." The man left the room never to be seen again. Barry was crestfallen.

Barry had a story that everyone loved. He would say, "Why would you and your wife travel scrunched up in the back of the plane, next to the toilet, flying tourist, when one day your daughter-in-law will travel first class!"

The audience would roar at this remark.

Usually, for the Naples seminar, Rita and I drove with Barry in his chauffeured limousine across Alligator Alley. One day, coming home, Barry bellowed, "I'm hungry. Let's stop for lunch."

Barry Kaye's all-time favorite food was a hotdog. I said, "Let's go to Costco, they have terrific hot dogs. And, I will pay."

Barry loved the idea of the Costco hotdog and the fact that I was paying. The limo double parked outside the entrance, and we all ate with gusto for about ten dollars. When we came out of the store, there was a large group of people surrounding the limousine. Never before had there been a chauffeured limousine outside of the Boca Costco store. I heard people say, "I think it belongs to Madonna or Tom Cruise or LeBron James!"

No. It belonged to the Jewish Billy Graham!

ARIZONA TO ALASKA

THE SOUTHWEST CAN be unbelievably hot during the summer. Rita and I experienced this heat when we went on a Tauck Tour to the Grand Canyon and the National Parks in 2004.

Staying at a resort in the Grand Canyon, we found the evening was cool and comfortable. I picked up a television station from Phoenix and listened to the weather report. The announcer said, "Tomorrow will be much cooler with the temperature dropping to 112 degrees. Today's high temperature was 121 degrees."

The Phoenix ladies would probably be taking out their winter clothes!

Traveling from the glorious Grand Canyon, we stopped for a break in Kingman, Arizona. It was brutally hot! Walking to the men's room with an elderly gentleman from Rhode Island, I remarked about the heat. Unbelievably, he confided to me, "Do you know who can't take the heat? The *fuckin'jews!* (said as one word). I was in the Army with them, and they would always pass out from the heat!"

I looked him in the eye and I said, "That's funny. You know, I'm a *fuckin'jew*, and I was in the Army, but I never passed out. And I was stationed in Saudi Arabia, and it was very hot. Also, my wife is a *fuckin'jew* so I better tell her not to leave the bus because she might pass out."

My elderly friend from Rhode Island hid from me for the next week!

***

To get away from the heat, the next summer we took a cruise to

Alaska. Being economical, I chose a room with no terrace, but only a port hole. Rita saw the room and went ballistic! She said it looked like we were living in a washing machine! She insisted that we change the room, and of course, I complied.

The cruise was great and Alaska was fun. We flew on a tiny plane over the glacier, and I noticed that the odometer read 50,000 miles. I asked the pilot if the plane was new, and he said, "Oh, no. This is a 1946 model and the odometer has gone around about eight times!"

We had lunch at a fishing lodge and I had the best salmon ever. We took a walk after our big lunch and came upon a large pile of doodoo. Rita said, "That must be one big dog."

I replied, "Does a bear shit in the woods?"

Rita took off and never ran so fast in her life!

ROCK 'N' ROLL IS HERE TO STAY

I WAS ALWAYS AN early Rock 'n' Roll enthusiast. When DooWop music started in 1955 with Alan Freed, I was its biggest fan. Going to Rock 'n' Roll shows with my friends at the Brooklyn Paramount Theater and listening to that music on WINS was the highlight of my teen years.

Now it's fifty years later and I'm living in Boca Pointe. The club announces that there will be a Rock 'n' Roll show starring the Drifters and the Coasters, and I'm excited to go. Both groups sang their famous songs. The Coasters sang "Charlie Brown" and "Yackety Yack"; the Drifters sang "Under the Boardwalk" and "Up on the Roof." But one thing was wrong; these were *not* the Coasters nor the Drifters. All the original singers would have to be at least in their seventies, while these imposters were all in their forties or fifties.

I was in the men's room and one of the Drifters came in. I asked him if he was an original Drifter, and he said absolutely yes. I told him, "I remember Clyde McPhatter and Ben E. King. I don't remember you."

He looked at me and said, "Man, you do know your f——g Rock 'n' Roll!"

He was right, I do know my f——g Rock 'n' Roll!

THE INLAWS

Rita's parents, both Holocaust survivors, were Orthodox Jews. Their narrow way of judgemental thinking, as with some Orthodox Jews, was that if you were not Orthodox, you're not Jewish. Unbelievably, I heard her mother actually say, that the worst Jew is better than the best goy!

They regarded me, a reform Jew, as a Catholic!

In 2005, the in-laws invited us to their big event, a Sunday night dinner at their new Orthodox synagogue in Deerfield Beach. The women were all bedecked in their newest clothes, definitely not bought at Saks or Neiman's. The men brought out their newest and shiniest walkers.

At exactly 6 p.m., the waiters brought out trays of appetizers. There was a mad scramble for the food, with wheelchairs colliding with walkers. By 6:05 p.m., most of the food was gone and several waiters were bloodied. More batches of food were brought out, and these little old people stuffed themselves!

Finally, we sat down to dinner, and after many speeches, the main dish was served. All at once, there was a giant flash of light as all of the women in the room took from their pocketbooks sheets of aluminum foil. No one in the room, except me, ate the main dish as the ladies all wrapped their overcooked broiled chicken in aluminum foil for tomorrow's dinner. Considering how it tasted, I should have done the same thing!

The orchestra started to play and people began to dance. Men danced with men and did the "Jewish Shuffle"; women did the same thing. I wanted to dance with my wife, but knowing that I would be thrown out, I sat in my chair and ate my gefilte fish.

***

Whenever he saw me, Rita's father always asked, "So, did you make any business today?"

***

Rita and I went on a Tauck tour to Eastern Europe in 2006. The trip was great as we visited Warsaw, Budapest, Vienna, and Prague. We took a side trip to Auschwitz, which was the most memorable part of the trip. Rita's mother was a prisoner there at the end of the war, and sadly Rita was visibly shaken. We had an international cell phone, and Rita decided to call her mother.

The call went like this: "Hi, Mom. Guess where we are; we're in Auschwitz. I'm standing outside the kitchen where you worked, building number five. What do you mean it's not building number five, where you worked; building number ten is something else."

The call went on like this and even though the surroundings were terrible, the phone call was really funny!

***

A couple of years later, Rita and I were on a Crystal Mediterranean cruise, and we stopped in the famous ancient city, Ephesus in Turkey. The local shops were really dinky, and they waited anxiously for unsuspecting American tourists. Rita was browsing in one store and came upon a shawl that she thought would be perfect for her mother. The shopkeeper told her it was fifty dollars and I laughed at him. The price was immediately dropped to forty dollars, but I told him, "No way," and we left the store because we were late for the bus. I told Rita that he would run right after us in the street, and of course, I was right. The shopkeeper asked me how much was I willing to pay, and I told him ten dollars. Surprisingly, he said okay, and he had already wrapped the shawl for us. I paid the shopkeeper and we got on the bus with the package.

Five minutes later, I realized that he just might have outsmarted me. I told Rita to open the package, and sure enough, there were two gaping holes in the shawl. I just knew that this wiseguy Turkish shopkeeper was laughing at how he had outsmarted an arrogant American tourist!

But the best part was that when Rita gave the present to her mother, despite the holes, she loved the shawl!

Rita and I overlooking Florence, Italy in 2008.

THE DISAPPEARING SUITCASE

JUST BEFORE OUR trip to Eastern Europe in 2006, I noticed that Bloomingdale's was having a huge sale on expensive luggage. Since I was always looking for a bargain, Rita and I visited Bloomies. Rita was always a top-of-the-line buyer, while I was more practical, looking for a deal. Rita found a great suitcase for me, of course, the most expensive in the store. However, this great suitcase was on sale at a fifty per cent discount. We bought it and both of us were happy.

The suitcase soon visited Warsaw, Vienna, Budapest, and Prague, and it certainly did its job. My fancy suitcase lived in my not-so-fancy garage. We were doing some construction work in the house, and my garage had visitors every day. Rita and I were going to New York in a few days, and she wanted to pack some things beforehand. I went into the garage to get my fancy suitcase, and I realized that it was AWOL!

Since we had so many people going through the garage over the past few weeks, it was hard to accuse anyone of stealing. The last person in the garage was my friend, Bill, the Water Doctor. I told him that my fancy suitcase was missing, and did he think that one of his men could be the culprit.

What he told me was really funny. He said, "It's impossible that one of my workers would steal your suitcase. I don't pay them enough to take a vacation!"

I bought my next fancy suitcase at Walmart!

TAKE THE MONEY AND RUN

Vanessa's best friend Julie got married in Washington DC in 2007. Rita and I had become friends with her parents, Susan and Ken, and so we were invited to the lavish wedding at the Ritz-Carlton Hotel. The wedding was great, as was our weekend in Washington.

As the formal wedding was winding down early Sunday morning, exhausted, we headed for our lovely room. In the elevator, a wedding guest complimented me on the silk pocket square that adorned my new tuxedo. The man said to me, "That's a great pocket square. I'd like to buy it from you. I'll give you one hundred dollars right now."

The silk pocket square was red, black, and silver in a paisley pattern. It was old; I think I bought it when JFK was president. I told the man that I had it for many years, and I just could not sell it.

The man answered, "I understand your situation, so I'll give you two hundred dollars for it."

I thought about his offer and considering that I only paid ten dollars for it, I replied cordially, "I appreciate your offer but just for sentimental reasons, I can not sell it."

Everyone else in the elevator was now getting excited about this impending transaction. Quickly, the man said, "Okay, I love the pocket square and I must have it. This is my final offer, take it or leave it — four hundred dollars!"

At this point, I really thought the stranger must be drunk and I did not want to take advantage of him, in his drunken condition. As the elevator door opened to my floor, I repeated, "Sorry, but it's just not for sale."

Rita disagreed with me ever so slightly. ***"Are you nuts"***, she screamed. "You turned down four hundred bucks for that rag?"

"That guy was so drunk, I just couldn't live with myself taking advantage of him," I responded.

The story continues. About eight years later, over the Christmas holiday, Vanessa and family came to visit Grandpa. Her now-married friend, Julie, invited us to lunch, at the Boca Beach Club. There was a big crowd at the Club, mostly young people, and I struck up a conversation with a nice guy, a contemporary of mine. We talked for a while and he told me that he was a guest at Julie's wedding eight years before. We both agreed that the wedding was terrific, and then I told him about the incident in the elevator. He laughed at my story and when lunch was over, we said goodbye and I headed home.

In the car, Vanessa was beside herself. She said, "Do you know who you were talking to? That's the man who wanted to buy your silk pocket square!"

I couldn't believe it. I have thought about that incident in the elevator many times over the years. Maybe I should have sold him the pocket square for four hundred dollars.

Woody Allen's first movie was called, *Take the Money and Run*.

Maybe that's what I should have done!

MY LOST CAR

MAJOR LEAGUE BASEBALL is a tough sell in South Florida. I think old people would rather go to a restaurant for a good meal than go to a baseball game and fall asleep!

The Yankees came to Miami to play the Marlins in an exhibition game just before the 2008 season began. Unbelievably, the stadium was packed with about 40,000 people; if they were playing Seattle that night, there would be about 4,000 people in the stands. Virtually everyone was rooting for the Yankees, and they were all wearing Derek Jeter jerseys.

I drove to the game with my friend Fred, a diehard Yankee fan. Ever since my early days in Brooklyn, rooting for the Dodgers, I hated the Yankees and I still do today. The Yankees won the exhibition game, but who cares.

We left the Stadium in the seventh inning to avoid the traffic going home, and I began to search for my car. I wasn't exactly sure where I had parked in this gigantic parking lot that was totally filled. Fortunately for me, I had a clicker that would turn the lights on in my car. Unfortunately for me, so did 40,000 other people, who also could not find their cars.

Lights were flashing everywhere. Car trunks were opening everywhere. It was quite a scene!By now, the game was over and the parking lot was jammed with people, all looking for their lost car. After about an hour of searching, we found my elusive lost auto.

I told Fred, "The next time I come to a baseball game here, it won't be against the Yankees but rather against Seattle. And I'll take the bus!"

SERENADING RITA

CELEBRATING RITA'S SIXTIETH birthday, in the summer of 2008, we went on a Crystal Mediterranean cruise. The luxury cruise started in Athens and ended in Nice. In between were stops in Turkey, the Greek Isles, Rome, and Florence.

We spent one morning touring Albania, a country that not many Americans have been to and for good reason — there's not a lot to see in Albania!

The cruise was absolutely first-class! Crystal, on their Mediterranean cruises, has a few formal nights where women wear gowns and men wear tuxedos. I brought a tuxedo with me and wore it twice. On the third formal night, after a hectic day of touring, I just did not want to get dressed up for dinner and wear a tuxedo. I was told that I absolutely had to wear it in the main dining room. I questioned them about not wearing formalwear by eating dinner downstairs in the casual buffet restaurant. Again, I was told that I must wear a tuxedo.

Exasperated, I demanded, if I order room service and eat it in my room, must I wear a tuxedo, or would be all right if I eat in my underwear?

The operator hung up on me!

***

The last night of the cruise meant that we had to get up very early the next morning and our luggage must be put outside our door by midnight. Rita was in bed reading, and I went downstairs to settle a bill. There were a few restaurants and lounges on the ship, and while waiting for the elevator, several musicians came out of the lounge. Being a practical joker, I saw a great opportunity here. I asked the group if they would do me a great favor to cheer up my wife who was sad that the cruise was over. They agreed and I led the four musicians to our room.

There was a guitarist, a violinist, a saxophone player, and a keyboard player. Rita liked the Spanish song "Green Eyes" ("Ojos Verdes"), and the group said that they would play it for her.

I opened the door, peeked in, and told Rita that I had a surprise for her. My small orchestra entered, surrounded the bed, and began to serenade my wife. Rita didn't know whether to laugh or cry or be angry at me for this intrusion.

Finally, she laughed and told me that this was the best part of the cruise. Today, I still miss that laugh!

The last great picture of Rita.
Jerusalem — 2012.

MY MAN OBAMA

THE LOCAL NEWSPAPERS displayed the headline in big print, *"Obama Coming to Boca Today."*

This was major news in October 2008, just before the presidential election. The Democratic candidate Barack Obama would be making a speech that day at B'nai Torah, a conservative synagogue in Boca. Tickets were impossible to get, but a friend of mine had a ticket that he could not use. He asked me if I would like to go to hear the candidate speak. At that time, I was intrigued with Senator Obama, and I was anxious to hear him, so of course I accepted the ticket.

I found a seat in the last row and considered myself lucky because it was standing room only. A woman approached me and asked if I would like to sit on the stage in the front of the room. I was wearing a suit and tie, and since most of the men there were wearing Boca outfits (shorts and t-shirts), I guess I looked dignified.

I told her that I would be happy to sit there, and she escorted me to the stage, minutes before the scheduled speech was to start. I noticed that there were television cameras all around and I had an idea. I found a seat right in the middle of the stage because I knew that the TV cameras would be focused on Senator Obama, and I would be sitting right behind him.

I quickly made a few phone calls, to friends and family, telling them to put on CNN in a few minutes, because Senator Obama and I were going to be on national television. The future president made a great speech and the large audience loved him.

I noticed the door from where he entered, and I realized that he would be exiting from the same door. When the speech ended, I maneuvered myself very close to that exit door. Sure enough, Senator Obama was slowly approaching the exit door, where I happened to be standing.

I shook his hand, told him I enjoyed his speech, and wished him luck in the upcoming election. All was good — everyone saw me on television and my candidate became president!

TOILET HUMOR

WHEN BARRY KAYE relocated his business from California to Florida in 1998, he was well known, mainly from doing seminars in South Florida over many years. His newspaper advertising was incessant, and he did a daily radio show on a local station. Finally, he tired of doing the radio show, and one day Barry asked Rita and me to do the program, on a permanent basis. Rita and I were novices when it came to radio, but we thought it would be a challenge and maybe a lot of fun, and perhaps a moneymaker.

Doing a live one-hour talk show was difficult, but we soon got the hang of it. Rita and I talked about life insurance, and more importantly — about life. I tried to make the show humorous and it worked. On days that they replayed past shows, I listened to myself and thought, *"Hey, that's pretty funny."*

Often people approached us and said, "Oh, you're *that* Rita and George. I love your show."

In Boca, we were minor celebrities!

Barry, his wife Carol, and Howard all thought the show was terrific. Carol said that we were the Jewish Tex and Jinx!

One morning Barry had a big sales meeting, and Barry and Howard realized that we needed a name for a new concept that we had just developed. Everyone came up with names that were quickly rejected by the bosses. But, yours truly, the Idea Man, came up with the name that was readily accepted and is still in use today!

Playing on the 401(k) plan, the new name was the ***401(KAYE) plan.***

***

Business suffered in early 2010, and I felt that we needed a terrific new ad campaign to shake things up. At that time, people were starting to sell their existing life insurance policies and replacing them with newer policies that were less expensive. I wanted to capitalize on that strategy. I had an offbeat idea that I thought would be great.

Picture a funny-looking man, sitting on the toilet with his pants pulled down. The caption read:

"Are you sitting with the best life insurance policy

available?

Or, are you just settling for number two?"

Everyone in the organization loved the ad. We ran a full-page ad in *The Sun Sentinel* anticipating a huge amount of positive feedback. We got phone calls all right, but every call was negative. What a disappointment!

My advertising career was definitely down the toilet!

PICASSO AND KARP

A s I HAVE stated before, photography is something that I enjoy, and with humility, I think that I am pretty good at it. My photos have been at several art shows, and featured at a local art gallery. Several of my pictures, I have printed, framed, and hung them all around my house.

After a vacation trip, I had two or three photos that looked good, and I asked Rita where did she think they should be hung. She rolled her eyes and said, "*More* pictures?"

Now I was insulted. I responded, "Do you think that when Pablo Picasso asked his wife where a new painting should be hung, Mrs. P. said, "Pablo, *another* painting?"

Rita got the message and said, "I think they will look great on this wall."

Thanks, Pablo!

OLIVER'S REPLACEMENT

THE RITZ-CARLTON HOTEL in Naples, Florida, was where Rita and I spent the July 4th weekend in 2011. Marlee, the lady who cleaned our house, watched Oliver, our white Bijon, who was thirteen years old and had just celebrated his "Bark Mitzvah!"

At 9 a.m., Marlee called to tell us that Oliver looked tired. Rita was concerned.

At 10 a.m., we received another call from Marlee to tell us Oliver had just died. Rita was now hysterical!

I told Marlee to bring the dog to our house, and we would be home soon. When we got home, Oliver was in the garage in a Nordstrom's shopping bag.

"Nordstrom's?" I said. "Oliver should be in a Saks or a Neiman's bag. How insulting to Oliver!"

Within a short time, we had another little dog — a red poodle. Rita allowed me to name the dog and I chose "Duke," named after my favorite Brooklyn Dodger — Duke Snider!

GRIEVING

A FTER MY WIFE Rita suddenly and unexpectedly passed away in July 2013, my children were very concerned about their dad entering into a state of depression. They investigated and found a local grievance group for seniors. I did not want to go to a meeting because I did not feel that I was depressed, but one day, not having anything to do, I reluctantly went.

This was the saddest looking group of old people that I had ever seen. Everyone sat in a big circle, and each person had to speak and tell their tale of woe.

The man sitting next to me spoke, and said that he had been married sixty years, missed his wife so much, slept with her underwear, and each night kissed her bra!

A woman told the story of diapering her sick husband for many years, and how much she realized that she totally enjoyed it! This was all a little too weird for me, and when I left, I realized that I was not depressed at all.

I left feeling a lot better leaving than when I came in!

GUCCI SNEAKERS

AT LONG LAST, I ended my business career in December 2014. In the past, people were supposed to retire at age sixty-five but of course I did not believe that, so I went on working another ten years. Now, I had too much to do — reading, writing, playing — and I finally realized that it was time just to hang it up.

Howard Kaye had his annual Christmas party at a restaurant and during the meal, I had an epiphany — I realized that now was the time to go. After lunch, I told Howard that the time had come for me to leave, and he became teary.

A few weeks later, Howard told me that a client had called looking for me. When he learned that I had retired, he asked, "Does George play tennis wearing his Gucci shoes?"

I liked that!

SENIOR DATING / KISSING FROGS

After Rita passed away in July 2013, my children, my sister, and my friends all gave me moral support. What I also received were many casseroles from the "Brisket Brigade" and a lot of introductions to a plethora of Florida's single women. After a while, I decided that I did not want to sit home by myself; I would rather sit home with someone. Years ago, I was told that for every single man in South Florida, there were fifty single women. It's true — and I got to know all of them and then some!

Dating lots of women at the same time became very confusing to me. I had to remember all the basic facts about each woman and that was hard. Divorced or widowed, New York or Philadelphia, many grandchildren or none at all, etc.

The day before my first date, I was pretty nervous. My daughter Heather called me and told me that she wanted to give me a pep talk. I told her, "I don't need a pep talk, I need Pepto Bismol!"

After all, I wasn't bad looking, I wasn't too dumb, my sense of humor wasn't bad, I could pay for dinner, I didn't have a jail record, and most important, I could drive at night. In other words, I was a quality man and a pretty good catch! But, truth be told, I felt kind of anxious that I was socializing so soon after Rita's death. I did not want to be seen in a local restaurant with a Boca Babe, so I chose to drive to a restaurant that was not really local. I'm not talking about driving to Jacksonville or Tampa, but rather to West Palm Beach or Fort Lauderdale. In a few cases in far out restaurants, I recognized some people and they saw me, and I became their topic of conversation. But who cares — me!

One interesting observation: My mother had gray hair, my aunts had gray hair, and my grandmother had gray hair. Can someone explain to me why all Boca Raton women, in their 60s and 70s, all have blonde hair. Maybe it's the fluoride in the water that reduces cavities that changes gray hair to blonde hair. Maybe all these Bleach Blonde Boca Babes go to the same beauty parlor. Since so many of these Palm Beach County Clones look exactly alike, perhaps they also go to the same plastic surgeon!

In baseball, prospects are rated in regard to five basic tools: They must be able to hit for average, hit with power, be strong defensively, have a strong throwing arm, and have speed.

In my view of a quality woman, she must have five basic tools:

A) Must be **nice,** kind, honest, compassionate, nurturing, romantic, upbeat, not weird (and laugh at my jokes).

B) Must be **intelligent,** worldly, educated, read the newspapers daily, (Harvard graduate a plus).

C) Must be **financially independent** (picking up a dinner tab is not frowned on).

D) Must be **good-looking,** (not necessarily movie star but maybe television star).

E) Must be **Jewish,** (please, not Orthodox).

***

I figure that this may be my last time around, and I want it to be with the perfect woman! In my quest for the perfect woman, I got to know many imperfect women:

1) I met a *Pretty Pompano* lady who possessed the five tools. Her fault was that she was divorced five times! I did not want to be number six.

2) A *Fabulous Fort Lauderdale Female* told me that she smoked pot. When I asked her how long she was doing this, she answered, "About fifty years." Not for me!

3) On a first date, I took a *Palm Beach Princess* to an upscale restaurant. She told me she was recently divorced, and very innocently,

I asked if she was friendly with her ex-husband. "He's an ass hole," she screamed, and everyone in the restaurant looked her way. There was no second date!

4) I was introduced to a *Magnificent Miami Miss* who told me that she was sixty-two, but I was doubtful about her age. During the course of the evening, she told me about her son who was a successful doctor. When I got home, I googled the son, which listed his age as fifty-one. Being pretty good at arithmetic, having a child at age eleven in Yemen is possible, but in Brooklyn, improbable!

5) From a dating site, I made a date with a *Classy Coral Springs Countess* who had a great picture. When I picked her up, I realized that the picture was ten years old. It was like the movie *Lost Horizon*!

6) A *Boca Babe* had her daughter's name tattooed on both forearms. She must've had a bad memory and could not recall her daughter's name!

7) A lady I knew introduced me to a woman who sounded terrific over the phone. In person, she was not terrific. I think that Pinocchio had a smaller nose than this *Bad-looking Boynton Bimbo*. I took her to a small out-of-the-way restaurant where nobody would see us. Of course, I was wrong and embarrassed when several people from Woodfield came over to say hello. Not a good evening!

8) Many years ago, we had a housekeeper from Barbados, and for my birthday, she gave me a shirt from her native country. I was very appreciative of her gift, but realistically, it was the ugliest shirt imaginable. I've kept this shirt all of these years and sometimes as a joke, I put it on for my kids. A *Marvelous Miami Madamoiselle* that I was dating, invited me to a fancy party so that she could show me off to her friends. She told me that everyone would be dressed up, and I should dress accordingly. As a joke, I wore my ugly Barbados shirt, and when she saw me, she screamed. I had clothes in my car, and I changed into appropriate duds and we went to her fancy party. I should have stuck with Barbados!

9) A *Boynton Beauty* told me that her father was a gangster who had spent many years in jail. She said that she knew many of his friends. I think that her last name was Capone!

10) A tennis friend, Glenn, told me that his wife had a friend who I would like. He showed me her picture, a *Frightful Fort Lauderdale Female* and I was not impressed. Glenn said that she was fun and she was frisky. I told him, no thanks, that my dog was frisky!

11) I went out with a very nice lady from the 'hood, a *Woodfield Wonder Woman*. Commuting was so easy, but there were negatives involved. It seemed that every person in Woodfield knew about this relationship, and it bothered me.

A wise man gave me this sage advice: "Do not date within your gate!"

12) A *Deerfield Doll* asked me if I was a "player." I knew that Lebron James was a good player, and I figured that being called a player was a compliment. So, when I told her that I was a player, she told me to take her home!

13) On a first date, over dinner, while eating my veal parmigiana, a *Boca Bombshell* told me that she loved me! I couldn't wait for dessert.

14) A *Delray Delicacy* told me that I was a "Serial Dater." Quickly, I responded that in the past I had worked in the Kelloggs factory, stamping expirations on Corn Flake boxes. Yes, I was a "Cereal Dater!" She thought that was funny and she proposed!

15) I had a blind date from hell with a *Plump Pompano Matron*. Besides having bad legs and a huge tush, this beauty ordered the most expensive thing on the menu, which she only nibbled on, and took the rest home for dinner. But the best part was that she was an arch conservative, making Sean Hannity look liberal! We certainly did not agree on political philosophy, and when she asked me about a second date, I told her that I would be vacationing in North Korea!

16) A *Winsome Wellington Woman* almost took the prize. Innocently, I asked her if she knew who was the president when she was born. Unbelievably, she answered, "How do I know? I was only a baby!"

Bye bye baby!

17) The best story was that I took out a non-Jewish lady, a *Delray Delight*, and to impress me with her Jewishness, she told me that she

had a friend who was a great pastry cook. "She made a SHALLA," my date said.

I made her repeat this three times and then I said, "You mean CHHHALLAH." She was embarrassed and I dropped her at the nearest bus stop!

***

I read somewhere that if you kiss enough frogs, a princess would appear. Well, I've kissed many frogs, but it's really not fun kissing frogs because they have bad breath!

Recently, I met a very nice lady who does not resemble a frog — hopefully, she is my princess! At last, finding the perfect woman would represent the final chapter in my life!

THE END

EXTRANEOUS PHOTOS

Jennifer's bas mitzvah - Jerusalem 1980 - Jennifer, Heather, Vanessa, Dad, Mom.

The Karp girls in London - 1984

Madison, Wisconsin - 1995
Vanessa's graduation from the University of Wisconsin

Surprise Party for George - 1994.
Vanessa, George, Heather, Rita, and Jennifer.

Another gala surprise party for Dad - 1999.
Rita, George, Heather and Jennifer.

Heather and Jordan get married!
Boston - 11/11/01
Darryl, baby Stella, Vanessa, Heather, Jordan, Jennifer, and Mark

Cousin Melissa and Kevin get married in Miami
Front - Jeremy, Stella, Elizabeth, Conrad
Back - Heather, Jennifer, Rita, George, Vanessa, Kathy and Arlene."

My three beauties - Jennifer, Vanessa, and Heather in 2016

Vanessa and her dad in 2017

Meet the Pearlmans
Mark, Jennifer, and Conrad in 2015

The Feldman family - mid 1990s
Harvey, Melissa, Arlene, Andrew, Matt, Jackie

The Epsein Ensemble - Los Angeles 2015
Heather, Evan, Jordan, Elizabeth

The Frank Family being honored in 2015
Jeremy, Darryl, Vanessa, Stella

MY FIVE BEAUTIFUL GRANDCHILDREN

Elizabeth, Conrad, Evan, Stella, and Jeremy.

Stella's bas mitzvah .

2014

***

THE END